Smugg
in Yorksmre

1700 – 1850

GRAHAM SMITH

COUNTRYSIDE BOOKS

NEWBURY, BERKSHIRE

FIRST PUBLISHED 1994
© Graham Smith 1994

Countryside Books
3 Catherine Road
Newbury, Berkshire.

ISBN 1 85306 238 3

The cover illustration, *Beach Landing,*
is from a drawing by Edward Dowden

Designed by Mon Mohan
Produced through MRM Associates Ltd., Reading.
Printed by Woolnough Bookbinding, Irthlingborough

Contents

A Victorian print which gives a rather romantic view of a smuggling affray.

Introduction

Smuggling was a vicious, violent and bloody trade even when judged by the brutal standards of the time. Corruption, intimidation, terror, brutality, torture, treason and even murder all played their part in the execution of the crime. The smuggling trade was operated on a massive scale and extended throughout the country, penetrating into every level of society. The smugglers were encouraged, supported and even financed by the local gentry. They were often protected by sympathetic magistrates, condoned and pardoned by many of the clergy. They were universally supported and assisted by the ordinary people and had the empathy of the local militia. In some areas their activities were facilitated by venal Customs officers. Then at times of war they worked hand in glove with the enemy and in return received utmost encouragement and active support. Very few smugglers paid the ultimate price for their crimes, most avoided transportation; impressment into the Royal Navy was invariably the harshest penalty they suffered. The goods that they smuggled found their way into virtually every household in the land from the most lowly cottage to the highest estate. The period from 1750 to 1830 has rightly been called the heyday of smuggling; at times and in some areas the countryside was virtually besieged by smuggling gangs. George Crabbe, the Suffolk poet who lived through the height of smuggling, wrote that the smugglers had gained 'a lawless passport through the land'.

Never before and never again would the country suffer such a prolonged state of utter lawlessness; the enormity and the violence of the smuggling trade surpassed any other form of illegal activity. So how did smuggling become so clothed in a mantle of cosy respectability and romanticised out of all recognition? The majority of people considered smuggling a fairly harmless pursuit and the only answer to unjust laws which imposed crushing and punitive duties on all luxuries and many of the necessities of life – tea, coffee, gin, tobacco, wines, salt, soap and candles. These laws were framed by a Government in which the people had no voice and whose burdens, they believed, fell unfairly upon them in particular. Without smuggling most, if not all, of these goods would have been priced far beyond the reach

5

A cartoon by William Heath depicting King William IV in the uniform of the Preventive Service.

of a large section of the community. Such laws inhibited their right to trade freely without the confines of high Customs duties and other import restrictions; hence those in the smuggling trade proudly called themselves free-traders. Smuggling, unlike most other illegal activities, thus came to be considered an honourable undertaking, because the only victim (or so people thought) was the Government through lost revenue. The payment of taxes, in whatever form, never has been and never will be a popular activity. More so in those days when most of the revenue financed expensive and distant wars and very little was used to ameliorate the wretched social conditions of the time. Most people felt that such duties and taxes had very little to do with them and their avoidance was considered reasonable and just.

Thus the smuggler stepped easily into a ready made role of folk hero – the good guy fighting an insensate and oppressive Government. The romantic views of the smugglers and their trade – moonlit coves, secret tunnels and caves, quaint inns and jovial, colourfully dressed 'gentlemen' – owe much of their origins to the many writers and artists who over the years have fostered such concepts. Novelists such as Sir Walter Scott, Blackmore, Cobbold, Hardy, Maude Falkner, Thorndike and Daphne du Maurier have all inculcated the romantic image of the bold, handsome and fearless smuggler. Artists as diverse as Sir David Wilkie, Rowlandson, Morland, Heath and 'Smuggler' Parker have left a graphic and highly idealised gallery of the smugglers and their trade, pictures which have been vividly impressed on the collective memory. In addition to this fund of written and visual material many smuggling myths originated first by word of mouth, were coloured on retelling and became gospel with the publication of broadsheets and popular songs such as *The Poor Smuggler's Boy*, *The Smuggler's Leap* and *The Attack on Dover Gaol*. However, it was Kipling's *Smuggler's Song*, first published in 1906, which is more responsible than anything else for perpetuating those romantic images of smuggling.

Having spent most of my working life in HM Customs and Excise I could be said to be biased in favour of the 'other side' – those unfortunate and much maligned Revenue officers of the time. However, I have endeavoured to present the smuggling trade in its true light through the use of Customs and Excise records, Parliamentary reports and papers, contemporary newspapers and accounts. From these the facts of the trade speak for themselves and need no fanciful embellishments to provide a rich, dramatic and colourful story of an activity which for over 100 years reached the proportions of a national industry.

Graham Smith
Chelmsford, 1994

1

The Smuggling Trade

Smuggling is a British pastime that can be traced back to the very first imposition of Customs duties and the establishment of Customs officials at the various medieval ports to collect those duties. The name itself is quite probably derived from the early English word 'smuckle', which in turn can be traced to the earlier Scandinavian words 'smugle' and 'smuggla', both of which have a similar meaning – to hide or a hiding hole. But the first recorded use of the word in English appeared in a State document of 1661: 'A sort of lewd people called Smuckellors . . . who make it their trade to steal and defraud His Majesty of His Revenue'.

The earliest references to smuggling or 'frauds', as the trade was then described, are to be found in the late 13th century, mainly because of the introduction of a swingeing new duty or 'Custom' on exported wool. This high export duty, which was equivalent to about 40% of the value, gave a great incentive to wool merchants to ship their wool and woolfells out of the country clandestinely. The Continent, especially the Low Countries, was eager to purchase the fine and high quality English wool, thus providing a ready and almost insatiable market for this English 'wealth', and so, unlike later smuggling, the early free-trade took the form of the illegal export of wool.

For many centuries the references to such smuggling tend to be rather spasmodic, occasional incidents are recorded in various State papers and there is no doubt that the trade continued apace, but there is doubt as to the extent. Several reasons account for this lack of information but perhaps the main explanation is that for long periods the Customs duties were 'farmed'. This was a system whereby the King leased out the collection of Customs duties at a port to merchants and financiers (mostly foreigners) on an annual basis. In return for the grant of these leases the King received an agreed quarterly sum, thus obtaining a certain revenue in advance without the additional expense of officers to collect it, except for the employment of one King's officer, a comptroller, to watch the King's interest! So frauds on the Revenue harmed the farmers' yield rather than the Exchequer. Indeed this system of farming the Customs can be considered as a very early example of privatisation.

Another reason for the lack of recorded evidence of early smuggling is that many of the Customs collectors at the ports were frequently prominent merchants in their own right. For instance Sir Richard Whittington (of pantomime fame) was a collector in London for several years, and in Hull the de la Pole family were involved in the collection of Customs duties as well as being important wine merchants. For such merchants, and there were many of them throughout the country, the wearing of two hats obviated the need to smuggle. Furthermore there was ample evidence of collusion between merchants and Customs officials. No port in the country seemed to be immune from Exchequer enquiries into a variety of frauds. For instance in 1417 the operations of the Hull Customs officers were closely scrutinised by Exchequer officials, and 30 years later there were investigations at York and Selby all relating to illegal shipments of wool.

During the Tudor age large increases in all import duties created a climate where import smuggling also became an attractive and profitable enterprise. But the organisation of the Customs service had been greatly reformed and improved. Strict conditions were introduced on the control of vessels, the limits of each port were clearly defined, the use of small creeks greatly restricted, and special legal quays were authorised for the loading and discharge of goods (except uniquely in the case of Hull). Masters of vessels were compelled to report all their cargo at the Custom House before discharge was allowed and similar restrictions were placed on exported goods. The overall effect of these new rules and regulations, at least as far as smuggling was concerned, was that if any vessel did not report, or was found discharging or loading goods at a time and place not approved by the Customs, its goods were considered to be smuggled just by those very facts. An essential element of the reforms was the greater supervision of Customs staff and encouragement for them to exert their powerful authority. There were troubles in all parts of the country as collectors attempted to enforce some semblance of control, but as long as recognised and legal trade brought the Exchequer a reasonable revenue the task of tackling the smuggling problem was put off until another day.

Towards the end of the 17th century the illegal export of wool or 'owling' was still the most urgent problem. The terms 'owling' and 'owlers' for the wool smugglers are said to be derived from their propensity to work at night, but more realistically the words are thought to be a corruption of 'woolers'. The owling trade, which had increased to massive proportions, was largely confined to Kent, Essex, East Anglia and Yorkshire. During 1669 the House of Lords debated the whole vexed question and evidence was heard of the number of owlers now employed in the trade who were said to operate in large well-armed gangs. A most ominous sign for the future was the number of 'fights and affrays between the owlers and Revenue men' presaging the violence of the next century.

The dramatic increase in smuggling can be attributed to two main factors. Perhaps the most significant was the introduction and development of the fore and aft rigging, which completely revolutionised sailing techniques, certainly as far as coastal waters were concerned. The dangers of strong tides, rock shallows, sandbanks, mudflats and the close proximity of the shore made the ability to tack and sail to windward of vital importance. This technical breakthrough had a marked effect on the growth of smuggling. Hitherto square-rigged vessels could only enter creeks on a favourable wind and would then have to remain there until the wind was in the right quarter to make their escape, thus making the chance of discovery that much greater. Small fore and aft rigged vessels could now sail into any creek, load or unload their illegal cargo and then leave swiftly, irrespective of the direction of the wind. Based on the successful design of Dutch yachts, small vessels were specially constructed for the smuggling trade, their main features were speed, lightness of construction, cheapness, manoeuvrability and shallow draft which enabled them to enter the smallest creek or inlet and operate close into the shore. Such vessels, with certain refinements, became the work-horses of the smuggling trade for the next 150 years.

The other major incentive to the growth of smuggling was a sudden and vast increase of import duties on a wide range of goods allied with the introduction of various trade restrictions and embargoes. These increases were largely as a result of the war with France, which demanded a large revenue to support the military. Tobacco, silks, lace, spices and brandy were now increasingly smuggled into the country. Inevitably, the greater the success of the smugglers the less the Revenue yield, which in turn only provoked further duty increases to make up the shortfall, and these provoked greater smuggling – a vicious circle that was replicated frequently over the next 100 years or so.

By the end of the 17th century a contemporary report described the owlers as 'a militia that in defiance of all authority convey their wool to shallops with such strength that the officers dare not defend them'. It was estimated that over 120,000 packs of wool were being smuggled annually. In 1699 a 'Landguard' of riding officers was introduced along the coasts and armed vessels were stationed at ports from Weymouth round to Whitehaven and from Newcastle right down to Wivenhoe in Essex. These appointments marked the birth of the Revenue fleet which for nearly a century and a half was second in size only to the Royal Navy. Smuggling had come of age and was now a nationwide problem.

Thus at the beginning of the new century the lines of battle had been drawn up for the desperate struggle that lay ahead. On the land there were the Customs riding officers and Excise officers, aided on rare occasions by the military; and at sea the Customs and the Excise vessels helped very infrequently by the Navy. For the next 130 years, at least, these forces would be at almost constant war with the smugglers with varying success. In less than a lifetime the face and extent of smuggling had drastically changed. The trade blazed throughout the country like a forest fire, no area was immune from the smugglers. Though the south coast from the Thames to Land's End was the most notorious area because of its closeness to the Continent, the east coast from Scotland down to East Anglia was also deeply involved in the free-trade, its smugglers looking to the Netherlands and Denmark to supply their goods. On the west coast from the Solway Firth to the Bristol Channel the smuggling trade was amply supplied from the Isle of Man and Ireland.

Not only the coastal areas were affected; the smuggled goods penetrated very far inland. In 1705 the Customs set up a force of land carriage officers, who were appointed to watch the coaching

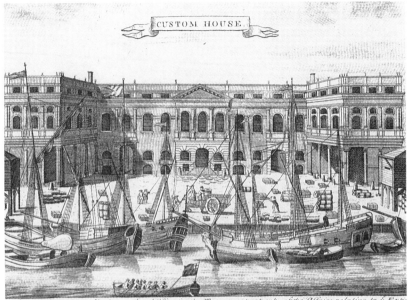

The London Custom House built in 1671 by Wren. This is where the Customs Board sat and made their decisions about smuggling policy.

inns and examine the various carriages on arrival to ensure that no smuggled goods had been carried from the ports. These officers also had powers to search the inns and warehouses and were moderately successful with seizures of silks, lace, bullion, playing cards and toilet waters – the most luxurious end of the market. There were land carriage officers at York, Newcastle, and Hull. On the other side of the coin, the hawkers, the packmen, the chapmen and the drovers ensured that smuggled goods found their way into virtually every town, village and hamlet in the country. Excise officers made frequent seizures miles inland, clearly demonstrating that the smuggling trade was a national problem. Smuggling had become a crime operated on such a grand and massive scale that all other forms of illegal activity – poaching, highway robbery and coining – paled in comparison.

The Customs, and to a lesser extent the Excise, struggled manfully to contain the enormity of the trade – it was a Sisyphean task.

Parliament continually introduced new legislation or reframed existing Acts in a vain attempt to combat smuggling. Each successive Act became more drastic and the penalties harsher with the result that the legislation became largely self-defeating. In 1718 the first 'Hovering' Act was introduced, which made any vessel under 50 tons laden with tea, spirits, tobacco or French silks found hovering within two leagues of the coast liable to seizure. Receivers of smuggled goods faced heavy fines or three months imprisonment and convicted smugglers seven years in gaol or impressment to the Navy. However, despite the mass of smuggling legislation the greatest problem that faced the Revenue forces was obtaining a conviction because generally the local magistrates sided with the smugglers. As for the more serious cases of armed assault and murder which were heard before local juries, few judgements were given in favour of the Revenue, most jurymen supported the smugglers either out of choice or out of fear. Indeed the perversion of justice became blatantly obvious with Revenue officers often finding themselves on trial for assault though in fact they had been merely trying to defend themselves from brutal attacks at the hands of the smugglers, who always vastly outnumbered them.

The first of many Parliamentary Inquiries into the smuggling trade sat in 1736 under Sir John Cope. Its report conveyed to Parliament (possibly for the first time in such strong and forthright terms) the state and extent of this incredible trade:

> 'The smugglers being grown to such a degree of insolence, as to carry on their wicked practices by force and violence, not only in the country and the remote parts of the Kingdom, but even in the City of London itself, going in gangs armed with swords, pistols and other weapons, even to the number of forty or fifty, by which means they have been too strong for the officers of the Revenue . . . The number of Custom House officers, who have been beaten, abused and wounded since Christmas 1723 being no less than 250, besides six others who have been actually murdered in the execution of their duty.'

This alarming report brought forth even sterner legislation which introduced the death penalty for hindering or wounding Revenue officers. As the legislation became increasingly Draconian it did little to combat the extent of the trade and, in fact, it actually exacerbated the situation. As capture automatically meant the

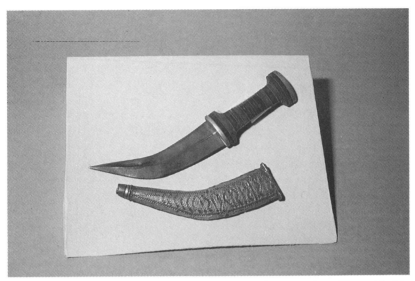

Vicious smuggler's knife found in a cave; the sheath is home made and has a thimble on the end.

A selection of arms used by the coastguard in the early 19th century.

death penalty, smugglers used far greater violence to ensure that they were not taken.

For sheer brutality and mindless violence the gangs that operated in Kent and Sussex were quite unsurpassed in the history of smuggling. Towns such as Lydd, Hastings, Deal, Dover, Folkestone and Rye were virtually in the complete control of smuggling gangs. They worked both night and day, often well over 100 strong, and they operated like small private armies terrorising the whole countryside. They were quite prepared to do battle with the Revenue and the military alike. They maimed and killed with a callous inhumanity, indeed nothing seemed too outrageous or dangerous for them to tackle. Gaols were attacked to rescue their colleagues and Custom Houses were broken into to retrieve their seized goods. Customs officers were kidnapped and transported over to France, where they were imprisoned until the Customs Board could arrange their release. Though other gangs operating in other parts of the country – the Browning family and the Saltburn gang in Yorkshire – were equally successful, the utter brutality and sheer violence was thankfully missing. There has never been an adequate explanation why Kent and Sussex should have produced such savage smugglers.

At sea the situation was just as desperate. By 1750 the vessels used in smuggling were so large and well-armed, and commanded with such verve and audacity – especially along the east coast – that they easily repulsed any attacks from Customs vessels and often treated them with utter contempt. As one Customs commander reported 'we are actually in danger of being run down and sunke by them, who have not only threatened to do so but also attempted it'. The smugglers were not intimidated by Naval vessels, they dealt with them in the same insolent manner, indeed they fought with even greater ferocity to avoid the dreaded impressment. Naval vessels therefore made little or no impact on the smuggling war, at least not until the end of the French wars. On the contrary there were instances of Naval officers and seamen being caught smuggling, so it can be said that relations between the Navy and the Customs were less than cordial.

The nature of the trade makes it virtually impossible to try to quantify the amount and value of goods smuggled or the disastrous effect on the country's legal trade and revenue. Although Customs collectors were often called upon to give

15

estimates of smuggling along their coasts, they were quite reluctant to furnish reports of large-scale smuggling as these might be construed as admitting a lax and ineffective control. Therefore all official figures of smuggled goods are likely to be underestimated and statistics of seized goods can also be misleading as they are very unreliable as a guide to the totals of goods smuggled.

However, in 1729 the Great Yarmouth collector reckoned that 49,000 half-ankers of brandy (roughly 180,000 gallons) were landed each year on the east coast alone. And just three years later the Treasury calculated that in one year 54,000 pounds of tea and 123,000 gallons of brandy had been seized in Kent and Sussex, though they thought this was less than 20% of the total smuggled. It is probably safe to surmise that in excess of £3 million of goods was being smuggled annually, at a time when the legal trade of the country amounted to some £12 million. The Treasury was therefore losing at least one quarter of its revenue and this figure may have been higher. It is now clear why duties were continually increased in order to replace this alarming deficit.

For most of the 18th century the staple commodity of the smuggler was tea (or dry goods as they called it). Legal tea was quite expensive, the East India Company had a monopoly of import and all tea sold legally in the country passed through its tea auctions in the City of London. Thus the combination of a trade monopoly and high import duties – both Customs and Excise – made tea smuggling a very profitable business. It was almost the perfect commodity to smuggle – easily obtainable on the Continent, light to transport and with a high value in proportion to its bulk. Much of the smuggled tea was bought in the Netherlands for as little as 6d to 1s per pound depending on quality. This tea could then be sold for anything from 4s to 10s per pound, when the cheapest legal tea cost 5s per pound. Even greater profits could be made by the judicious use of dyed leaves (rosemary was a favourite) to adulterate the tea, quite a common practice. By 1750 it was estimated that over three million pounds of tea were being smuggled annually, more than three times the legal trade, and just 20 years later the smuggled figure was thought to be in excess of seven million pounds.

In 1784 one of William Pitt's first measures on becoming Prime Minister was to reduce the import duty from an equivalent of

125% to a mere 12½%. With this one stroke he made tea smuggling virtually unprofitable, though it was still brought into the country as ballast! However, during the long war with France the duty on tea slowly increased until it was back in favour with the smugglers. Perhaps the one good thing that came out of tea smuggling was that though at the beginning of the century tea was a fashionable but expensive luxury enjoyed by comparatively few, by the end of the century it was in common use even in the households of the very poor. A nation of tea drinkers had been born!

Tobacco, since its first introduction into this country, has always been heavily taxed, so by the same token it was the most smuggled commodity for well over 300 years. In the 18th century it could be purchased for as little as 3d per pound on the Continent and sold in this country for 1s 3d to 1s 6d a pound. Quite a lot of the smuggled tobacco had been first imported legally with the duty paid but on exportation this duty was then repaid, only for this same tobacco to find itself back in the country illegally landed! The Humber estuary and Hull, in particular, had a thriving tobacco smuggling trade well into the present century.

During the interminable wars with France all French goods were totally prohibited, so items such as silks, lace, handkerchiefs, gloves, glassware, playing cards, perfumed waters and brandy were at a premium and the smugglers could name almost any price as there were no legal goods to act as a comparison. There was a famous *cause célèbre* when Lady Holderness was caught at Dover in possession of 114 Parisian silk dresses. However, this conviction did not deter her, for when her husband was made Governor of the Cinque Ports, she operated a private smuggling venture from Walmer Castle in Kent supplying French silks, furniture and porcelain for her society friends. French brandy was one item that had a ready market in this country. It could be obtained in the Channel ports for as little as 1s 6d to 2s 6d a gallon and Parson Woodforde of Norfolk recorded in 1800 that he paid his smuggler '21s a gallon'.

But without doubt the most smuggled spirit was geneva or gin, sometimes called Hollands. The word is derived from the French 'genevre' or juniper – the flavouring used in its manufacture. This spirit, which was Dutch in origin, was first introduced into the country by William III. At first it was slow to catch on in this country but when the English distillers found how easy it was to produce they flooded the market with the cheap drink. Within a short time the sales of gin had far exceeded those of beer and ale. By the mid 18th century there was so much gin drinking that it had become a grave social problem. Excise duty on spirits was vastly increased in a vain attempt to control consumption but only acted as an added incentive to the smuggling trade. Special distilleries were set up on the Continent merely to supply the smuggling trade. Geneva could be bought for as little as 1s per gallon and sold from 4s to 6s a gallon. Furthermore it was brought in at well over proof and needed to be diluted to make it potable; this only added to its attraction to the customers who felt they were getting their money's worth. By the end of the century geneva had achieved respectability as a middle-class drink, largely as a result of the smuggling trade.

The whole of the smuggling trade was very profitable for everyone, from the financial backer right down to the merest labourer. It could even be argued that it was equally advantageous to the other side. The seizure rewards for the Revenue officers could be quite large, though there were very few officers who managed to retire in comfort on the proceeds of seized goods. In the early years of the century smuggling was mainly conducted on an *ad hoc* basis and comprised fishermen turning to the trade to eke out a poor season, but as soon as it was realised that the trade was hugely profitable, smuggling became a highly organised and most professional affair as befits a large and thriving industry.

Those who financed the purchase of the smuggled goods were often long-established and outwardly respectable traders and merchants in the community, and many local gentry were quite prepared to back the smugglers. Often the local Customs officers had strong suspicions about these shadowy godfather figures but had no evidence, nor indeed were they likely to get any, to proceed against them in law. The financial backers almost always acted through an agent who dealt directly with the master smuggler, agreeing the percentage profits and what goods his principal and his friends required. The funding of smuggling was considered no different to any other venture investment. It was estimated that by the 1770s over £1 million in coin was being exported each year just to pay for the smuggled goods, though in 1770 William Hickey, whilst on board a returning East India vessel in the Channel, witnessed a smuggler taking delivery of a variety of goods for which he then calmly paid by means of a cheque for £1,200 drawn on a London bank! Certainly after the Napoleonic Wars much of the payment for smuggled goods was arranged by bankers' drafts – just the same as the legal trade.

The shipmaster who arranged the purchase and brought over the goods in his vessel was paid handsomely for what was a small risk – at least in the early days – when there were relatively few Revenue vessels and most of the seizures were made on land. He was essential to the whole smuggling operation, first for his contacts in the French and Dutch ports, which enabled him to purchase goods at competitive prices and then more importantly for his expertise as a 'spotsman'. His innate navigational skills and intimate knowledge of the local coast meant that he could bring his vessel as close as possible to a pre-arranged spot, where the landers were waiting. In many cases he operated without contacts on shore, quite prepared to sell his goods to passing vessels or local fishermen.

However, the largest share of the profits was taken by the master smuggler on land. It was he who arranged the unloading, dispatch, storage and ultimate disposal of the goods, and he who took the greatest risks, but the profits were so large that it was suggested he could afford to lose two cargoes out of three and still make a profit. The logistical problems in managing a successful landing were formidable and needed a person of exceptional organisational flair as well as good leadership qualities – motivation by fear did play a part but it was not the whole answer. Getting sufficient landers, animals and carts to a given spot, planning the various routes to be taken, pre-arranging storage bases and subsequent deliveries to the customers were large tasks, especially as they were normally undertaken during the hours of darkness, on rough and inferior paths and with the constant threat of a Customs ambush. Though the prime motivation was money, there is no doubt much truth in the view expressed by Dostoevsky that a smuggler 'works from inclination. He is on one side an artist, he risks everything, runs terrible risks and gets out of scrapes and sometimes acts with a sort of inspiration. It is a passion as strong as gambling'.

Such were the main principals in the affair. The supporting cast was made up of landers, tubmen, look-out men and batmen, who were normally recruited on a nightly basis from the labouring 19 poor of the port and were, more often than not, farm workers. Generally they would receive 10s to 12s for a few hours' work as well as a free dollop of tea and maybe some geneva. With the average wage for a farm worker at 8s to 10s a week, smuggling was a most tempting proposition. It was said that farmers close to the coasts had considerable trouble finding enough men to work the land, especially at harvest time. The smuggling master demanded utter loyalty and a conspiracy of silence if they were unlucky enough to be caught, although in fairness their families were usually well looked after should they be gaoled.

The tubmen had the most physically demanding job of all. They were employed as human packhorses to carry two half-ankers of spirit slung over their shoulders. Thomas Hardy tells of an old tubman in Dorset who remembered 'the horrible suffocating sensation produced by a pair of spirit tubs slung upon the chest and back after stumbling with the burden of them for several miles inland over rough country and in darkness'. These poor men were the real drudges of the trade, and ran a far greater risk of capture; many ended up in gaol for months if not years as Crown debtors, and many more were impressed into the Navy.

The batmen, as their name implies, carried bats – 'stout wooden staves' often iron-tipped and at least five feet long. They were used to ward off the swords and the cutlasses of the Revenue men and were also very effective weapons, especially to unseat men on horseback. They were, in essence, the security guards employed to protect the valuable cargo and to assist the nucleus of regular gang members, who always rode well armed with pistols, swords and loaded whips.

To complete the picture, the smugglers received almost universal support from the rest of the community. At the very minimum this meant maintaining complete secrecy about smuggling operations. Farmers quite willingly left their stables and barns conveniently unlocked to allow the smugglers to 'borrow' their horses and carts. Packages of tea and gin were left when their property was returned. Women often took an active part in the proceedings; it was suspected but not proven that smugglers' wives in Beer, Devon had attacked a riding officer and thrown him to his death from a cliff top. Though Richard Cobbold's highly romanticised 19th century novel of a Suffolk woman smuggler *Margaret Catchpole* was supposed to have been based on true facts, there is no hard evidence to support the story.

During the latter decades of the 18th century the most important and successful means for the suppression of smuggling were the Revenue vessels. They now numbered 45 and operated from Newcastle right round the coast to Whitehaven as well as in Scotland and Ireland. Most were clinker-built (with lapped planking), of very strong construction and with a great sail area for their overall size. The main feature of these vessels was the bowsprit, which was almost two-thirds the length of the hull to give the vessels extra speed: indeed some that were built at the turn of the century were said to be the fastest vessels afloat. For the next 50 years they took the war to the smugglers and the majority of the large seizures of smuggled goods were made by them.

With the advent of the long and bitter war with France in 1793, all hopes of a reduction of duties to alleviate the smuggling situation quickly disappeared. All Customs and Excise duties were increased and new ones were introduced for good measure. As the war dragged on so the duties escalated to fund the ruinous costs of waging war on land and at sea. For instance by 1815 tobacco duty had risen to 3s a pound – almost three times the amount at the outset. Also tea duty mounted steadily again until it reached 96%. Although all trade with France was strictly forbidden, French brandy and wines were still being drunk by the upper classes of society including members of the Government without any apparent conscience! With so many Revenue vessels seconded to Naval fleet duties and few dragoons left to assist the Customs, the coastline was left to a mere handful of riding officers and the odd preventive boat as the only defence. High duties, near-siege conditions and a sadly depleted Revenue service were ideal conditions for an upsurge of smuggling.

The French government actively encouraged smuggling. Despite the war smugglers were given free access to the Continental ports, most of which had areas of quays specially reserved for the English smuggling vessels. The French urgently required English gold coins; it is doubtful whether they could have paid their armies without a steady influx of gold. It was estimated that about £10,000 in coin was being smuggled out of the country each week. Equally important to the French was the information about defences and the movement of vessels that the smugglers brought with them. Many smugglers saw the sale of such information as an added bonus, and like many intellectuals in this country were in favour of the changed political regime in France. The 'letters for a spy' carried by Kipling's smugglers was not too far from the truth. Napoleon commented during his exile on St Helena:

> '. . . All the intelligence I received from England came through the smugglers. They are likeable people and have courage and ability to do anything for money . . . They are *genti terribili* . . .'

Equally it must be said that many smugglers served with distinction in the Navy when they were impressed; many acted as pilots. Certainly nobody could question the fact that they were very fine seamen.

In an attempt to strengthen the coast defences, in 1809 a new Revenue force was established called the Preventive Waterguard (the name survived in the Customs and Excise until the early 1970s). This body of men was intended to link up the existing forces – the cutters and the riding officers. The new force would operate near the shore and tackle the smugglers that had managed to run the gauntlet of the cutters further out to sea. The Waterguard, as the name suggests, was provided with small rowing galleys to patrol the shores regularly. The new preventive men were normally stationed away from their homes to avoid any possible collusion with relatives or friends. The coastline of England and Wales was divided into three districts, each controlled by an Inspecting Commander, who had overall command of the Waterguard and the cutters in the area. The three inspectors were selected from the most experienced commanders. The new system was designed to provide a cohesive control of all the anti-smuggling forces, at long last the Customs were beginning to get their act together!

During the next few years there were the first signs of a gradual change in smuggling methods. Reports, few and isolated at first, of smuggled goods being hidden in specially concealed compartments on vessels began to appear in the Customs records. This trend became more prevalent over the next 30 years as the old romantic type of smuggling runs on the shore became less and less frequent, although it must be stressed that the change did not appear overnight, there were still many bitter battles to be fought on both land and sea.

In February 1816 the Preventive Waterguard was moved away from the Customs and placed under the control of a Royal Navy captain, who was given strict orders to reorganise the service on Naval lines and to introduce Naval discipline. Recruitment for the service was placed in the hands of the Admiralty, who also had control of all the cutters. At the stroke of a pen the Customs and Excise services were rendered virtually devoid of any anti-smuggling forces. In addition a special 'Coast Blockade Force' solely manned by Naval personnel was established along the Kent and Sussex coasts.

There was no doubt that the new measures had their desired effects with some moderate successes, but unfortunately it was at a great financial cost. Nearly 7,000 people were employed in the various forces at an annual cost of well-over £ ½ million and yet there was still a certain lack of co-operation between the forces with many instances of duplication of effort. The Treasury, ever keen to obtain value for money, felt it was high time to re-examine in detail the various services involved in the prevention of smuggling. Never had one subject been so deliberated on or taxed the minds of so many public servants.

The committee appointed to study the problem expressed its grave concern at 'the most flagrant degree of audacity and violence of the smugglers and the considerable quantities of spirits and tobacco introduced from the other side' – not particularly original comments as it had all been said many, many times before. The committee also highlighted the lack of central control of all the preventive services. It recommended that the Preventive Waterguard be returned to the control of the Customs Board, the force of riding officers be reduced to a mere 50 men and all but the very largest Revenue vessels be returned to Customs control.

The report was approved and with effect from 15th January 1822 the new preventive establishment – the Waterguard, the cutters and the riding officers – were amalgamated into one force under a new name, the Coast Guard (the two words were separate for a number of years). Though the force was under the direction of the Customs Board, it was headed by William Bowles, a Royal Navy captain, and in future it was decreed that all the officers and men appointed to the service would be nominated by the Admiralty, thus establishing the long tradition of Naval principles   23 within the Coastguard.

The early encouraging successes of the Coastguard forced the smugglers to seek more ingenious methods to hide their goods. The wooden sailing vessels were particularly suited to a variety of concealments – hollow bulkheads, false bows, double bottoms in cabins, false ceilings, as well as goods being hidden in coils of rope, sails, cargo and ballast. The variety seemed infinite and as soon as a new concealment was discovered, full details of the method were circulated to every port. The avenues of communication were improving!

As for smuggling by passengers, this type of trade appeared to be flourishing, judged by some of the seizures recorded at the various packet ports in the 1830s. They reveal a bewildering range of goods – silk stockings, earrings, leather gloves, chips (strips of wood for making hats), lace, snuff boxes, inkstands, clocks, wine-glasses, eau-de-Cologne, petticoats, playing cards, watches, musical boxes, fans, porcelain, false teeth, feathers, endless articles of silk and lace clothing and, of course, tobacco, French brandy and wines. In those days each vessel had to produce a passenger list and when the passengers landed they were shown into a waiting-room and were called forward to identify their luggage. The Customs officers complained 'Lady passengers are dressing themselves in valuable dresses and jewels, more calculated for their entry into a drawing-room, than merely to come ashore. They are all items newly acquired abroad'. The steady rise of petty smuggling by passengers would continue throughout the century as foreign travel became no longer the sole privilege of the upper classes. The Chairman of the Customs Board thought 'it would be very unfair to call upon parties to declare whether they had goods liable to duty or not, and to subject them to a severe penalty if they made a false declaration'. One can only ask, why not? A fine example of the duality of Victorian morality – 'ordinary' smugglers were still liable to hefty fines and even transportation for very minor smuggling offences.

In 1831 the authorities suggested that the Coastguard should become 'in all its branches essentially Naval'. From this time forward all recruits were trained at Naval establishments and were required to serve on Naval vessels, abroad if necessary. It thus became, in essence, a Naval reserve force with the prevention of smuggling a secondary part of its duties. Indeed, during the

Crimean War over half its officers and men saw active service. At the same time the organisation of the riding officers – now known as the Mounted Guard – was drastically altered. All new entrants were to be aged under 30 years and to have served in a cavalry regiment.

The battle at sea between the cutters and the smuggling vessels had altered to one of a 'cops and robbers' chase. The majority of smugglers no longer sought to fight it out with the cutters but mostly now cut and ran at the first sight of a Revenue vessel. The smuggling vessels would often jettison their cargo, not solely to lighten the vessel for greater speed but also to avoid being caught redhanded. Even if they were subsequently apprehended by the Revenue it was very difficult to prove in a court of law that the recovered cargo had actually come from the captured vessel. Furthermore the cutter commanders were under strict orders that their first duty was to secure the smuggled goods; thus many a smuggling vessel escaped despite the fact that it might have lost all its cargo.

The smuggling trade at this time gives an impression of a game of hide and seek played on a grand scale. The smugglers attempted to gain information on the timing of Coastguard patrols and the movements of cutters and several Coastguard men were court-martialled for passing on such information for gain, whilst the Revenue men or 'Philistines', as they were now commonly known, were desperately trying to buy information on the movements of smugglers. At least it could be said that smuggling had now become civilised.

There can be no doubt that the Coastguard and its force of cutters – nearly 50 in number – and ably abetted by the Customs officers at the ports – were achieving a very marked success. However, despite the obvious increased efficiency and more and bigger seizures, the greatest single factor in the reduction of smuggling was the steady lowering of import duties and the introduction of free trade. Way back in the 1770s Adam Smith, the famous economist and Scottish Customs Commissioner, had maintained that the only real answer to smuggling was the reduction of punitive duties and at long last his views were being vindicated.

The leading proponent of laissez-faire was Sir Robert Peel. He was an ardent believer in the removal of all trade barriers and the reduction of restrictive import duties. In the four years from 1842 to 1845 no less than 1,200 articles were freed from import duties. By 1851 there would only be 48 articles liable to duty and ten years later a trade treaty with France drastically reduced the duties on French brandy and wines as well as exempting many French goods from duty. The only goods that brought in any appreciable revenue were sugar, tobacco, tea, wines, spirits and timber. The illegal trade in wines, tea and silks virtually ceased when the profit margin became so slight that smuggling was no longer worth the risk. Sugar as a commodity had never lent itself to smuggling, not even in the heyday of the trade, so the only goods which remained worth smuggling were spirits and tobacco, but spirits, largely because of their bulk and smaller profitability, were smuggled far less. For the rest of the century the main and almost only commodity smuggled was tobacco. For some unaccountable reason the north-east of the country appeared to be the most notorious area for this trade. Both the Tyne and the Humber estuaries figured very large in tobacco smuggling, coming mostly from Holland, Belgium, Prussia and America.

All vessels arriving at the ports were suspect. Tobacco was concealed on regular trading vessels, either in the crews' accommodation or in the holds; although with the advent of steam vessels the engine rooms became favourite hiding places. With so many goods now duty free one of the tricks of the trade was to hide tobacco in these goods. Coasting vessels, which normally would receive scant attention from the Customs, were greatly involved in the tobacco trade. Quite often tobacco was overstowed with bulk cargoes such as coal, grain, apples and fish.

In 1851 collectors at every port in the kingdom, as well as all inspecting commanders of the Coastguard, were asked to report the extent of smuggling in their areas over the previous ten years. There had been only 70 large-scale smuggling runs in the decade – on average just seven a year – throughout the country including Scotland and Ireland. In nearly one third of these runs most of the goods had been recovered, many smugglers were arrested and a fair number of vessels, carts and horses seized. These figures present an overall picture of a greatly declining trade.

The Coastguard in 1850 comprised over 6,000 men and had no less than 70 cutters of various sizes operating around the coasts – all at an annual cost of over £½ million. The review of smuggling throughout the kingdom suggested that some reduction could be

Smugglers Attacked. A popular early 19th century print by an unknown artist.
(By kind permission of Alan Hay).

made in the size of the service without greatly endangering the
Revenue. There was a sharp reduction in the land force and over a
quarter of the cutter fleet was disbanded. Despite this depletion of
the Coastguard there was no evidence of any material increase in
smuggling during the period. The Government now recognised
that the protection of the Revenue against smuggling was only one
of the many reasons for the existence of the Coastguard. The
defence of the coasts in case of invasion, acting as a Naval reserve
and life-saving duties were all considered more important than
anti-smuggling duties. Consequently, in 1856 the control of the
service was transferred from the Customs to the Admiralty.

27

This decision was not greeted with enthusiasm by the Customs Board, in fact they made very strong representations to the Treasury on the wisdom of such a change, and were clearly informed that the responsibility rested solely with the Government and that the Customs Board would stand 'entirely exonerated, if any inconvenience arose to the detriment of the Revenue'. In short, if smuggling increased as a result of this measure it would not be the Customs' fault – a rather enviable position to be in! From 1856 no Customs officer has carried arms though the Coastguard men remained armed for many more years, mainly for their role in the defence of the coasts.

Despite all their previous misgivings the Customs Board were able to produce an encouraging report on smuggling just a year later:

'With the reductions of duties and the removal of needless and vexatious restrictions, smuggling has greatly diminished and the public sentiments with regard to it have undergone a very considerable change. The smuggler is no longer an object of public sympathy or a hero of romance, and people are just beginning to awaken to the perception of the fact that his offence is less a fraud on the Revenue, than a robbing of the fair trader. Smuggling proper is now almost entirely confined to tobacco, spirits and watches . . . all these cases are on the decrease and in the last ten years have diminished to about one-third.'

Although clearly smuggling had not ceased, it had been greatly reduced and what remained had emerged in a vastly different format. However, Hull and the Humber estuary continued to pose a smuggling problem right into the next century. The long battle with the smugglers that had been waged nationwide over the previous 150 years was finally won. It could now be safely said 'The gentlemen had gone by'!

2

The Impact on the Yorkshire Coast

From the towering and rugged headlands of the north, interspersed as they are with secluded and picturesque bays, along to the splendid chalk cliffs of Flamborough Head with its spectacular caves, the broad sweeping sands of Bridlington Bay and right to the quiet plains of the south, the Yorkshire coast has scenery to rival any in the land. Almost 120 miles in length, it is a coastline of unsurpassed beauty. To the interior are the Cleveland Hills, the North Yorks Moors, the Wolds and the wide emptiness of Holderness, making the whole area one of rare natural beauty.

Since 1974 boundary changes have desecrated the ancient East and North Ridings of the county. The area to the immediate north of Staithes has been absorbed into the new county of Cleveland, whereas in the south the area surrounding Hull has become known as North Humberside. However, for the purposes of this book I, like many other writers, have ignored such changes and have treated the Yorkshire coast as commencing at the estuary of the river Tees, the old boundary with County Durham, and ending at the Humber estuary in the south. In effect what the majority of people would recognise as Yorkshire whatever Government bureaucrats have decreed to the contrary!

The whole of this coast has a very long and rich maritime history which is proudly proclaimed from Hull in the south to Redcar in the far north. The exploits of the fishermen, the whalers, the shipbuilders, the collier masters, the lifeboatmen, Captain Cook and, of course, the smugglers are quite rightly praised and honoured in splendid local museums and exhibitions along the whole of the coast. These proud traditions of Yorkshire ships and seamen can certainly match those of any other stretch of coastline in the country.

The Romans were the first to recognise the vulnerability of this wild stretch of coast to raids and invasions from 'savages' from across the sea, and they established a series of warning signal stations on high vantage points along the coast. Some of the ruins have survived and those we are aware of were sited at Hunt Cliff (near Saltburn), Goldsborough, Ravenscar, Scarborough and Filey. There may have been others which have now been lost to the ravages of the sea, but there is no evidence of a line of Roman forts similar to those they built further south in East Anglia, as part of their Saxon shore defence system. After the departure of the Romans, the coast and land suffered frequent violent incursions by a succession of invaders – Anglo-Saxons, Norsemen and Vikings from across the Mare Germanicum (German Sea or Ocean) as it was then known; in fact a map as late as 1828 still showed it as the German Ocean rather than as it is known today – the North Sea. These raids and later permanent settlements have left their indelible marks on the various names found along the coast; ness – a headland, scarr – a long rocky ledge, and wyke – a creek or bay. Indeed the name Humber is said to be derived from a legendary King of the Huns, who invaded the area long before the Romans.

To understand the smuggling activities of any area, it is necessary to have some concept of how the various ports developed, what areas they serviced, what were the normal (legal) trade patterns and the type of coastal traffic. Merchant and fishing vessels, as opposed to those solely employed in smuggling, needed some feasible reason or excuse for being in the area should they be intercepted by a Revenue vessel. This is even more important with Yorkshire smuggling because, unlike the south and East Anglian coasts where the distances to France and Holland and the Channel Islands were relatively short, the sea route from the Yorkshire coast to Holland – the nearest foreign country where goods could be obtained – was long and fraught with dangers. To sail to Holland entailed a round trip of over 400 miles and to challenge the North Sea was a formidable task, nor was smuggling an activity that was only practised during the summer months. Furthermore for much of the sea route back to Yorkshire the smuggling vessels had to run the gauntlet of Revenue vessels and at times Naval vessels. There are many instances of Yorkshire vessels being seized off East Anglia, but most of their smuggled cargoes, I believe, were destined for their home coast. This was a very real danger as the East Anglia and Kent coasts were strongly protected by large and heavily armed Revenue vessels. By the beginning of the 19th century the Customs Board had also established an efficient information system in most Continental smuggling ports and the information supplied by these correspondents was precise, particular and speedy. Therefore the longer the return journey the greater the risk of detection and detention.

Such prolonged and dangerous journeys would seem to militate against much smuggling activity along the Yorkshire coast, and there was not an obviously large market for the smuggled goods, unlike East Anglia and the south coast where the majority of the goods ended up in London. Much of the Yorkshire coast was relatively sparsely populated and even the interior of the county was not particularly populous with the possible exception of the area close to Hull. The Yorkshire coast therefore might seem a rather unlikely area for large-scale smuggling but this was not so; the Customs records of the Yorkshire ports give ample evidence of the extent of smuggling. The Customs collectors were constantly reporting the helplessness of their plight, the impossibility of controlling the vicious trade without an adequate number of officers, Revenue vessels and the deployment of troops. Nevertheless it would be foolish to imply that the Yorkshire smuggling trade was as active, extensive or, indeed, as violent as that on the south and south west coasts, but its free-trade was of a sufficient scale and volume to produce its own smuggling legends and folk-heroes, evinced by the number of smuggling stories and inns along the coast, as well as the presence of a couple of smuggling museums.

For centuries the maritime trade of Yorkshire has been dominated by its three main ports – Whitby, Scarborough and Hull, with Bridlington as a late developer. Somewhat strangely they are relatively equally spread in distance along the coast, but this is pure coincidence as their growth and development was due mainly to natural reasons.

Whitby can lay claim to be the oldest existing port in Yorkshire. It can trace its origins back to pre-Roman days. Situated on the wide estuary of the river Esk, the only river between the Tees and the Humber to flow into the North Sea. In the Dark Ages it

Kings Chest: similar to the one provided for Whitby Custom House.

became a Christian centre of major importance and the medieval port was developed to support the Christian community. Until the beginning of the 18th century Whitby was a harbour almost totally devoted to fishing, but its fame and prosperity grew out of shipbuilding and whaling. As Daniel Defoe commented '. . . an excellent harbour . . . they build very good ships for the coal trade, and many of them too, which makes the town very rich . . .' The port had an enviable reputation for building strong and reliable vessels with large storage capacities and very economical to operate. The Whitby collier brig or 'cat' was designed to carry about 600 tons of coal and they were used almost exclusively in the Newcastle coal trade, though Captain Cook, whose memory is still kept very much alive in the town, did adapt them for his voyages of exploration.

By the end of the 18th century Whitby had become the sixth port in the kingdom based on trade and shipping figures, larger indeed than Bristol, and most of this increase was due to whaling. Specially strengthened collier brigs went forth to the Greenland fishery and returned with the profitable cargoes of oil, whalebone and whalemeat – it was one of the most important whaling ports in the country. However, the port's pre-eminence was rather short-lived; when whaling died in the 1830s it returned to its previous existence as a fishing port – as it is today. Though much of the former glory of the port has long since vanished, it still retains that special aura of the sea and ships – a proud heritage of fishing, whaling, shipbuilding, Captain Cook and, of course, smuggling!

Some 18 miles south of Whitby lies Scarborough. This elegant and spacious cliff-top town manages to combine a fine meld of history, spa water, seaside resort and a busy working harbour. But it was noted for its safe and sheltered anchorage long before it became famous first as a spa and then as a precursor of the English seaside holiday. The headland makes its south bay a natural harbour and it is thought that the Vikings developed this potential and built the first quay; there was certainly a quay here in the 13th century. In 1323 Scarborough was a staple port – authorised by the King to export wool and woolfells. Over 300 years later, in 1696, that intrepid lady traveller Celia Fiennes found it to be '. . . a very pretty sea-port built on the side of a high hill . . . all one side of the Castle stands out to the sea-shore a good length, it's open to the main ocean and to secure the harbour there is a mole or half-moone, two, one within, the other something resembling the Cobb at Lime' [Lyme Regis].

Towards the end of the 18th century the port was a scene of thriving and bustling activity, its merchants owned the largest number of collier vessels in the country and it vied with Whitby in the number of vessels built, though not quite achieving the same high reputation as its near neighbour. It had now become the tenth busiest port in the country. There was always a large fishing fleet at the port – both inshore and deep-sea – and a busy foreign and coasting trade to support the luxury tastes of this select and prosperous town, which claimed to be the 'Queen of Watering Places'. Side by side with its rapid development as a spa and superior seaside resort was the busy harbour, somewhat divorced from the town high up on the hill. Here the mix of seamen and fishermen were not averse to a spot of smuggling as the old Three Mariners Inn on the quayside testifies. The harbour still attracts thousands of summer visitors and it is often crowded with trawlers, drifters, cobles and mules.

From time immemorial the Humber estuary has been an important commercial waterway giving access to the sea for the rivers Hull, Ouse, Trent, Wharfe and Don. In Roman and medieval times many of the towns situated on navigable stretches of these rivers became ports of some consequence. York was a major Roman port, coals and wines in and wool and corn out. Hedon, Selby and Beverley all had a considerable foreign trade, mainly in timber, coals, wine, wool and corn. It is a popular misconception that York declined as a port during the 14th century but when Defoe visited the city in the early 18th century he found '. . . the river so navigable and so near the sea, the merchants here trade directly to what part of the world they will, for ships from sixty to eighty ton and under come up to the very city . . . they carry on a considerable trade, they import their own wines from France and Portugal and likewise their own deals and timber from Norway and bring their own coals from Newcastle and Sunderland'. But when he arrived at Hedon he thought it 'a little pleasant town – having a little haven from the sea, which threatens Hull that it will in time grow up to be a great place . . . but I fear that their haven will do nothing considerable for them unless they can do something very considerable for that'. Silting, a tragic fire and fierce competition from Hull completed the demise of this ancient port which in 1200 could boast more than a mile of quays.

Considering the mercantile significance of the Humber estuary, it was fairly obvious that whichever town dominated this seaway would eventually grow into a major port. York, largely due to its distance from the sea, lost out as vessels grew in size. One strong contender was the medieval port of Ravenspur situated close to the mouth of the Humber. In 1323 it was a place of some consequence with its own Customs collector responsible for more revenue than either that of York or Hull. It is now solely remembered as the port where Henry IV landed in July 1399 before he was crowned King. Ravenspur cannot be found on any map, it has long since disappeared under the sea, a victim of the coastal erosion which is a constant problem on this part of the coast.

Hull can trace its origins back to the 12th century when the monks of Meaux redirected the river Hull to form a small harbour and establish a village called Wyke-upon-Hull. Its subsequent growth owes much to Edward I, who acquired the village, fitted it out as a Royal harbour, granted it a charter and renamed it Kings-town-upon-Hull. The main reason for the harbour was the export of wool and woolfells from the rich pastures of the hinterland. By the 17th century Hull had virtually monopolised most of the trade in the area. It was intimately connected with Scandinavia, the Baltic, Russia and, most of all, the Netherlands. Defoe likened the port to 'Hamburgh, Dantzich and Rotterdam ... there is more business done in Hull than in any other town of its bigness in Europe ...' Much of this business was conducted in the flourishing and influential Merchants' Exchange – other than Bristol – the only one outside London at the time.

By the end of the 18th century Hull had become the third largest port in the country servicing the fast growing industrial hinterland via the Ouse and the Trent rivers. It was a premier shipbuilding port and also competed with Whitby in whaling. For most of the century this vast trade was conducted from the ancient wharves clustered around the town centre. One visitor described the scene as '... hundreds of masts like a forest ... and the smells of timber, tar, fish and hemp mingled with spices, tea, coffee and wines ... the noise and bustle was tremendous ...' For some inexplicable reason in 1559 the town had been exempt from the Act enforcing ports to provide 'proper legal quays' for the discharge and loading of foreign goods. Then, in 1774, the town was ordered to regularise the position, though 'the old staiths Thomas Walton's Shipyard and Rotten Herring used from time immemorial may still be used for landing and shipping on condition they are fitted with proper quays ...' Just four years later the first dock was opened. The port continued to grow at a phenomenal rate, as well as having a large foreign trade it had the biggest fishing fleet in the world. Though still deeply involved in

35

the Northern trade and Holland, it extended its traffic to America, the West Indies and the Far East, its exports almost exceeding those of London. Hull is now the only major port on the Yorkshire coast and is still amongst the top six ports in the country.

Besides the three big ports, the coast has several old towns which were largely involved in fishing. Bridlington benefited greatly from its sheltered position in the lee of Flamborough Head, its bay had for centuries been considered the safest anchorage along the whole of the east coast. Thus the small fishing town prospered as a port of refuge for storm-bound vessels until it was successfully developed into an important deep-sea fishing port as well as a seaside resort of some note.

In the north of the county there are several natural bays and havens sheltered from the ferocity of the winter storms, which with the addition of stone breakwaters and quays have enabled them to support active fishing communities. Much of this type of fishing disappeared with steam trawlers and these delightful and attractive harbours – Runswick Bay, Robin Hood's Bay and Staithes – now attract tourists in their thousands every summer. One Customs collector commented in the 18th century 'Show me a fisherman and I will show you a smuggler'. And certainly these small Yorkshire harbours were rife with smuggling.

The traditional fishing boat of the Yorkshire coast is the coble. For centuries these unique vessels have been vital to the fishing industry along the whole coast. The design of the coble is closely based on the Viking longship. They are flat-bottomed, clinker built with a mast and single sail but also fitted for rowing with at least three pairs of oars. They can vary in length but in the smuggling days they mostly seemed to be at least 19 feet and manned by six or more men. The cobles have a high powerful bow, a deep forefront and a rudder extending four feet or so below the keel. Designed particularly to cope with the heavy North seas and to be launched and beached on unprotected sands even in the most difficult seas, they are excellent sea-boats able to cope with the worst weather, and many Yorkshire fishermen stoutly maintained that they would prefer to be out in a storm in a coble than a lifeboat. In fact it was in a coble that Grace Darling went out on her historic and intrepid rescue attempt.

36   During the 18th century the cost of a coble ranged from £17 in

the 1720s to £21 by the end of the century. They were relatively inexpensive and considering the enormous profits to be made in the smuggling trade it only needed a couple of successful runs for the cobles to pay for themselves. Also, if they happened to be seized by the Customs the financial loss was not too catastrophic. The other side of the coin was that because of their low value the Customs men received very little in seizure rewards for cobles, especially as the Crown claimed half of the value of any seized vessel. The Customs at both Whitby and Scarborough had their own cobles to enable them to patrol close inshore where the larger Revenue vessels dare not venture.

Cobles were in use in all the recognised fishing villages along the coast and because of their design and sturdy adaptability they were able to turn any stretch of sand into a fishing and therefore a smuggling harbour. Places such as Saltburn, Sandsend, Filey, Redcar and Flamborough were ideal for the use of cobles. In 1914 there were said to be no less than 70 operating from Flamborough, and at Filey today these somewhat flat-bellied and multi-coloured vessels can be seen at the 'Coble Landing' near the lifeboat house. During the heyday of smuggling there were literally hundreds of them sailing the inshore waters of the Yorkshire coast from every port, harbour or bay and most, if not all, were involved in the smuggling trade. Indeed they were so suited to smuggling that one could imagine they had been specially designed for the trade.

One other maritime activity on the coast is worthy of mention as it did have some bearing on smuggling activities in the area. The majestic cliffs to the north of Scarborough yielded a variety of minerals and perhaps the most developed was alum shale. In the 18th and early 19th centuries it was used in the manufacture of Epsom salts, the dyeing of wool, the sizing of paper and in printing. Ravenscar Bay, a few miles north of Scarborough, was developed purely for the alum trade. Its small harbour and quay were used by vessels bringing in coal for use in the mines and then loading the alum. Sandsend, just north of Whitby, was really the centre of this thriving trade, with well over 100 vessels using its harbour annually. One of the problems for the Customs was that there was a coastwise duty on coal so they were compelled to employ an officer known as a 'coalmeter' to weigh the coal, charge and collect the duty. One unfortunate Whitby officer was stationed at Boulby Allom Works. Boulby cliffs rise to almost 700 feet, the highest point along the Yorkshire coast, and the alum house was situated at the bottom of a narrow ravine in the rocks where vessels came to discharge and load their cargoes, with the greatest difficulty I am sure. This must have been the most lonely and depressing Customs post along the whole of the coast. The Customs authorities found it almost impossible to control the sheer volume of small vessels employed in the alum trade; they certainly brought in more than coal!

The topography of the Yorkshire coast in all its infinite variety has had a most marked and positive effect on the smuggling of the area. The impressive and dramatic nature of the coastline has largely dictated the type of free-trade activities undertaken. Any study of smuggling throughout the country clearly shows that smugglers, if nothing else, were very skilful and resourceful in not only overcoming the natural features of their shores but also adept in using them to their best advantage. This innate ingenuity is demonstrated by the manner in which the Yorkshire smugglers operated most successfully on what is such a rugged and demanding coast.

One of the most interesting aspects of smuggling in Yorkshire is that it encapsulates all the different methods and practices. To most people the word 'smuggling' conjures up images of a sandy shore with goods being landed and loaded onto teams of horses or ponies, whilst just out to sea the smuggling vessel rides at anchor. This is indeed the most accepted view of smuggling and such 'runs' as they are called were most prevalent on the wide open shores of East Anglia, Kent, Sussex, Hampshire and Dorset; they were obviously better suited to such landings and were without doubt the most active and thriving smuggling areas. And it is perhaps no coincidence that the most prolific smuggling along the Yorkshire coast took place on the broad and sandy shores to the far north of the county near Redcar and Saltburn and to a lesser extent on the flat plains of Holderness.

The firm and flat sands of the shoreline from Coatham to Saltburn were ideal for these old-style smuggling runs. Also in the days before the Victorian development of this coast it was relatively uninhabited save for the odd fishing village and the Customs records of the period are full of references to runs or landings along this stretch – always *after* a successful run had taken place!

The best known and most successful (as far as is known!) Yorkshire smuggler – John Andrew – operated from Saltburn in precisely the same manner as the more famous (or notorious?) smugglers of the south coast of the country. Andrew would have been totally conversant with the kind of large smuggling operations mounted by Isaac Gulliver, Arthur Gray and Henry Carter, among others. Not only was the coast ideal for the trade but it was helped in the distribution of the goods further inland by the nearby industrial area of Teesmouth, rapidly growing in population and providing an eager market for the smuggled goods, and the busy market town of Guisborough.

Although Holderness has certain similarities with the Saltburn coast, for instance it possesses equally fine, flat sands – much longer though not so firm – it is given over more to sand dunes, which were used to hide goods. Holderness was probably an even more deserted coast and during the winter rather prone to flooding. It was certainly not an easy stretch for the Customs to patrol and control though they were well aware of the dangers it posed. Riding officers were stationed at Skipsea, Owthorn and Hornsea, and it was here that the Supervisor for all the riding officers south of Bridlington was based. It was perhaps not such a well-used smuggling haunt as the north of the county because of the permanent presence of dragoons at Beverley, about twelve miles inland from Hornsea and within easy riding distance of the coast. Also, except for Beverley there was a lack of any sizeable population to support the trade. Perhaps there was an even simpler reason – no single individual of the calibre of John Andrew to organise the free-trade activities! This might be borne out by the fact that when Andrew was finally caught by the Customs he was undertaking a smuggling run near Hornsea. Indeed the last known large smuggling run on the Yorkshire coast took place in July 1846 at Hornsea. Even when this type of smuggling was disappearing the Customs collector at Bridlington considered that 'no part of the coast of England affords greater facilities for smuggling . . . to prevent which requires a strong force, with a constant supervision'!

Compared with the large quantities of goods that were landed on these open and deserted sands, the volume of goods brought into the small fishing and alum ports was considerably less. Nevertheless the trade was regular and landings were frequent – at least 39 to judge by contemporary Customs reports. Indeed these ports presented a constant and considerable problem for the Customs throughout the heyday of smuggling as the small villages were squeezed into the narrow confines of the natural breaks of the coastline and were quite inaccessible. Furthermore they were close-knit communities solely devoted to fishing and every member was somehow involved in the trade, either by assisting the landing or hiding the smuggled goods in their cottages, which still cling precariously to the steep cliff sides. Men, women and children were involved in moving the goods either to Whitby or further inland, where the farmers and their labourers encouraged and assisted in the operation. At the alum workings hordes of largely itinerant miners provided an enthusiastic work-force glad to assist in the landings, as the extra money earned for a night's work provided a much needed supplement to their meagre wages. Staithes, Sandsend, Skinnigrove and Runswick Bay were all thorns in the side of the Whitby Customs and despite riding officers being stationed at or near these villages, there was too scant a number of seizures to warrant their employment. Several officers tried to justify the situation with the argument that their very presence in the village had produced a strong preventive effect, but this was rarely accepted as a valid excuse and the scale of smuggling certainly suggested otherwise.

But above all the rest Robin Hood's Bay stands out as *the* smuggling village along this stretch of coast. Without a shadow of doubt it can be said to have been a community almost solely devoted to the free-trade. In 1817 it had five large fishing cobles crewed by five men and no less than 36 smaller cobles with six oars whereas at that time Scarborough had just three large cobles and Whitby only two. The wide bay was used by large smuggling vessels and the Baysmen went out in their cobles to bring ashore vast quantities of goods. The fiercely independent fishermen – hardy and excellent seamen in all weathers – knew their coastal waters intimately and the Revenue boats and men were no match for them. The goods, when landed, quickly disappeared into the cellars and specially constructed hiding places in the cottages that huddled along the narrow lanes and passageways of this quaint and fascinating village. It was boasted that smuggled goods could be moved from the bottom of the village to the top barely seeing the light of day – it must have been a game of hide and seek on a

40

grand scale – so frustrating for the Revenue forces. Perhaps more than any other village along the coast, Robin Hood's Bay had a long and unenviable reputation for hostility to outsiders. Even as late as the beginning of this century Leo Walmsley, the novelist who grew up in the village, vividly recalled this strong antipathy to 'foreigners'. Indeed one wonders just how the various Customs officers and their families managed to live and survive in such a hostile environment, though it must be said that there is no evidence of any violence directed at them, unlike the more brutal and ruthless smuggling towns in the south of the country – Deal, Hastings, Rye and Poole.

The Humber estuary has a long tradition of smuggling; there is evidence that as far back as the 13th century wool had been smuggled out of the country from the cluster of small medieval ports of the Humber. The number of small creeks that line the banks of this wide and long estuary – Hull is some 20 miles from its mouth – encouraged the landing of goods by vessels before their arrival at Hull. They were not necessarily the usual smuggled goods – though these did get landed by this method – but were often timber, hemp, market goods and even coastwise coal. For this very reason the Customs have always employed vessels to cruise the estuary in an attempt to prevent and curtail such abuses. One collector in the 1840s maintained that 'although such illegal landings are diminishing, they still are of sufficient number to warrant our boatmen maintaining a vigilant watch along such creeks and shores . . .'

The proximity of the docks to the town made the landing and sale of smuggled goods a relatively simple and safe operation; this fact is borne out by the number of seizures of smuggled goods made in the streets, houses and inns surrounding the quays. An early Hull historian claimed that there were 'vast caverns running under High Street into the town' and it was in this area that the prominent Hull merchants lived. The regularity of vessels, both British and foreign, using the port and trading to and from Holland and the Baltic countries, ensured that valuable contacts could be made and maintained with the merchants and traders in the port and quite often goods were smuggled to order. There was even an instance of a seizure of German porcelain – not something that would normally be brought in for pure speculation! This type of smuggling was virtually impossible to 41 contain and control. When large docks with formidably high walls were being constructed in other major ports – London, Liverpool and Glasgow – the town docks at Hull were quite open, which only further aided the illegal landings of goods and caused endless problems for the Customs men at the port. In one rather cheeky incident a Danish seaman was actually caught in the act of selling some smuggled tobacco right opposite the Hull Custom House!

There was one very special feature of smuggling in the Humber estuary and that was the staggering amount of tobacco illegally landed. Judging by the number of large seizures this was a trade of vast proportions especially if it is accepted that only a small percentage of the total (maybe 20 to 25%) was ever seized by the Customs. From the 1820s onwards much of the smuggling in Hull was undertaken by ships' crews hiding the goods in cabins, engine rooms, forepeaks, bulkheads and in the cargo itself. Some of these concealments were very clever and required long and laborious 'rummages' – to use the Customs term. The trade in smuggled tobacco continued well into the present century long after large-scale smuggling had petered out in most other areas. Certainly the Humber, with Hull in particular, has always been known as a prime smuggling area.

One of the undeniable axioms of smuggling is that for the trade to flourish and prosper there must be a ready market for the goods to be sold in considerable quantities to finance such a risky and expensive enterprise, and the Humber estuary offered unrivalled access to the heavily populated industrial areas of South Yorkshire and the North Midlands. The small river boats and sailing barges that plied their trade along the rivers Ouse, Trent and Aire greatly aided the speedy distribution of smuggled goods, as did the working canal barges. Excise officers often seized smuggled goods as far inland as Leeds, Sheffield, Doncaster and Retford and most, if not all, had come from Hull or elsewhere along the Humber.

There was a fair number of large and heavily armed smuggling vessels operating off the Yorkshire coast. These professional smugglers – if such we may call them, for that's what they were – obtained their supplies of geneva, brandy, tobacco, wines and tea directly either from the Netherlands or France; ports such as

Flushing, Ostend, Dunkirk and Calais specialised in providing goods for the English smuggling trade. Many English merchants had established 'houses' in these ports solely to trade in smuggled goods, and so highly organised was the whole business that letters of credit and bankers' drafts were accepted for payment as well as hard cash. So important was the smuggling trade to the ports that even during the long Napoleonic wars English smugglers were still allowed free entry. Tobacco was packed in small waterproof containers, as was tea. Spirits and wine were sold in special half-ankers (3½ gallons) for ease of landing and carrying, and there were even special distilleries established at Dunkirk and Schiedam to produce geneva solely for the smuggling trade. East India goods – tea, coffee, spices and silks – could be obtained in both the Netherlands and Denmark at less than one sixth of the legal duty paid prices in England. In July 1752 all east coast collectors were warned by the Customs Board of 'a recent auction of East India goods in Copenhagen . . . you should therefore expect large quantities of tea to be run and watch all vessels from Denmark with utmost vigilance' – far easier said than complied with!

Another prime source of smuggled goods was the number of Dutch and French privateers that operated off the Yorkshire coast. Since the Tudor days the 'dread of Dunkirkers' put the whole coastline in fear. In 1699 a heavily armed French privateer captured the captain and crew of a Whitby vessel and then calmly and insolently sailed into the harbour demanding a ransom of £200 or else! During the 18th century these large and well-armed vessels entered the smuggling trade. They hovered along the coast selling goods to passing colliers, coasting vessels and fishing cobles, the latter coming out to rendezvous with them. Rarely did they attempt to land the goods themselves but appeared to have an unspoken agreement to assist and protect any English vessel in trouble when trying to land the goods. However, on their return home they were not averse to capturing the odd stray collier to add further profit to an already lucrative voyage. Right up until the present century large Dutch vessels, which were virtually floating supermarkets of duty-free goods, followed the fishing fleets of the east coast ports and supplied them with cheap tobacco and spirits. These coopers as they were called, only disappeared with the outbreak of the First World War.

There is sufficient Customs evidence to show that the colliers   43 in the Newcastle to London 'sea cole' trade indulged in quite a bit of smuggling. Several colliers were confiscated off East Anglia after being caught in the act and more than a few Customs collectors expressed their suspicions of 'the Newcastle coal vessels'. It is probably not too surprising as on their arrival in London they freely mingled with vessels from all over Europe and the Americas, and there were ample opportunities to speculate and dabble a little in the free-trade. Any extra money this would bring was welcomed by most seamen in the coal trade who received about 30s to 35s for a round trip to London, which could take more than a month. Much depended on the colliers' masters' view of the free-trade. Some took to the business whole-heartedly, others merely condoned it, while many forbade any association with the trade and strictly enforced their precept. It is not known whether James Cook indulged during the six years he served on a Newcastle collier!

The number of vessels involved in the Newcastle coal trade was really quite staggering. Even in 1698 Celia Fiennes at Scarborough commented '. . . all the Shipps pass to go to Newcastle or that way. I see 70 saile of Shipps – supposed to be colliers . . .' Just 100 years later it was said there were 597 vessels in the trade and all of them at some time or another passed along the Yorkshire coast. This stretch of seaway was so busy that it could rightly be called the 'M1 of the sea'. Indeed many of the crews came from Yorkshire ports and they and their fishermen colleagues took full advantage of the situation, arranging smuggling transactions that greatly profited them both.

Besides the colliers there were many small coasting vessels which were involved in the smuggling trade. Some merely plied to nearby ports or just along the Yorkshire coast, others were regular visitors to London and what could be more natural than they should be used to distribute smuggled goods. On the very odd occasion when the Customs, more by luck than judgement, seized goods on them, the quantities involved were really quite trifling – the odd drop of brandy, a couple of pounds of tobacco or maybe a few bottles of wine – really very minor infractions considering the enormous quantities that were being landed elsewhere. However, the mere knowledge that smuggled goods were being moved in this manner made Customs work all that more frustrating and it really meant that every single vessel – be it

THE IMPACT ON THE YORKSHIRE COAST

large or small - was suspect, quite a daunting and depressing prospect!

And how did the Revenue forces in Yorkshire organise themselves in their attempts to control and suppress smuggling on such a scale? First of all it must be recognised that the Customs and Excise were then two completely separate services operating quite independently of each other and with different priorities. There was a considerable amount of rivalry between the two services and frequent bitter disputes broke out in the ports over the rights of first search of vessels and the sharing of rewards for seized goods. The Excise officers generally considered themselves a cut above mere Customs officers and they also felt that they were more efficient and effective. Certainly the Excise service was far better managed and was relatively free from corruption.

The Excise, though its main involvement was with duties on home produced goods such as beer, malt, candles, soap, salt, bricks and gin, was also concerned with smuggling. Excise duties had been imposed (in addition to Customs duties) on a wide range of imported goods, for instance tobacco, spirits, wines, coffee and tea; in fact the Excise duties on spirits and tea were far greater than those of the Customs. There were Excise 'port officers' stationed at Hull, Scarborough and Whitby to collect these duties and in each of the ports there were separate Excise warehouses to store imported goods. Most of the Excise officers were based inland and invariably at market towns – Guisborough, Stokesley, Pickering, Great Driffield, Scarborough, Bridlington, Hornsea, Beverley, Selby, York, and, of course, Hull. Most, but not all, of the Excise clashes with smugglers were inland and there is an instance of an Excise officer being murdered by smugglers near Scarborough.

But it was the Customs service that really bore the full brunt of the smuggling trade with the occasional help of troops and, even more rarely, the assistance of Naval vessels at sea. Most of the Customs officers were stationed at the main ports. They worked from the Custom House, which was normally sited in the most prominent position in the port and was virtually the focal point of the maritime community of the port. Long before the establishment of shipping exchanges, the Custom House was the meeting place for merchants, shipowners and masters to discuss and exchange views on commerce and to seek information on all aspects of the shipping and trade of the port. The Customs staff themselves, especially the collectors, were important members of the maritime community; they had wide powers and carried no small influence in the development of the port.

From 1671, when it can be said that the Customs department came of age, with the establishment of a Board of Commissioners, the staffing complements at the ports were based solely on the shipping and trading activities of each port. It must be remembered that the *raison d'être* of the officers was the collection of duties on imported and exported goods, this was their main and essential responsibility and the prevention and suppression of smuggling was a rather secondary matter. Indeed as the scale of smuggling increased dramatically during the 18th century the Government preferred to strengthen the legislation and increase the penalties for smuggling rather than provide sufficient resources to control the illegal trade. It is very noticeable that when extra Customs officers were finally and rather grudgingly provided, they were always too few in number and much too late because by that time smuggling had passed beyond any reasonable control; then it would have needed an army to contain the trade – a virtual civil war!

The Customs officers at the ports had to cope with a variety of activities other than the collection of revenue and the prevention of smuggling. Their other duties were many and varied, ranging from health and quarantine control, the registration of British ships, salvage of wreck, immigration and emigration, passenger control, the enforcement of trade embargoes (especially at times of war), whaling and sea fishery controls, and the collection of trade statistics and lighthouse dues. They were also involved with the administration of the dreaded press gang on behalf of the Admiralty. There were several land-based press gangs operating in Yorkshire at Hull and Whitby. Then, in 1795, the Customs were handed another responsibility – the infamous Quota Acts which were introduced for 'the provision of able bodied men to serve His Majesty in the Navy of Great Britain". Under these Acts Yorkshire as a county was compelled to find 1,081 men (the largest number in the country) and *in addition* each port was required to supply a set number of sailors (Whitby 573, Scarborough 275, Bridlington 50 and Hull 731). These figures show the relative importance of the Yorkshire ports; only London,

Liverpool and Whitehaven had to provide more seamen. The Customs' connection with the impressment of seamen and the Quota Acts only heaped more opprobrium on their heads and increased (if indeed that were possible!) the antipathy and hostility of the community in general.

The port of Stockton-on-Tees has been included because for much of the period covered by this book the collector there was responsible for that stretch of Yorkshire coast from the river Tees to Huntcliffe Fort, which saw so much smuggling activity. For a large part of the time there was only one riding officer in the area to cover the 20 or so miles of shore. He was based at Marsh or Mask (Marske-by-Sea), though later another officer was appointed to Coatham. Not until 1775 did the port have any Revenue vessels – not even a small coble! According to the collector 'the difficulties of navigation of this river makes their employment of no practical use'. However, he failed to explain just how merchants' vessels managed to negotiate such a dangerous waterway or indeed more importantly how the smuggling vessels made their way to Yarm – several miles upriver – without too many problems! An example of how local management almost seemed to go out of its way to help the free-trade.

The jurisdiction of the Whitby collector went from Skinningrove in the north to Robin Hood's Bay, about five miles to the south of the port. There were riding officers at 'Lofthouse' (Loftus), Staithes, Sandsend and, of course, Robin Hood's Bay. There had always been at least one Revenue coble at the port, although in the 1710s the Customs Surveyor had been forced to provide a small coble at his own expense because the Customs Board had refused point blank to fund it! Their argument was that 'the port and estuary was too small and did not require the use of a vessel'. In those days the main, if not only, reason for a boat was to visit the vessels on arrival at the port, they had not even been considered at that time for anti-smuggling duties.

The collector at Scarborough controlled Filey and Ravenscar with officers at both places, as well as a riding officer at Burniston, just a few miles north of the town and at Hummanby to the south. Because the two harbours at Scarborough were considered compact, the collector considered that 'the revenue is not disadvantaged by the lack of a vessel but what is needed is the 47 presence of a heavily-armed cutter to cruise the coast'. At least it can be said that he had the right idea.

But it was the Bridlington collector who had the longest coastline to protect and guard; it stretched right from Flamborough to Spurn Head, with a permanent officer at Flamborough and several riding officers patrolling the Holderness shores. It is interesting to note in passing that Benjamin Milne, who was collector in 1806, was so distressed and concerned at the number of shipping disasters near Flamborough Head (174 vessels lost from 1770 to 1806) that he strongly petitioned Trinity House for a lighthouse to be erected 'about 400 yards from the extreme point of the promontory'. So convincing was his proposal that within six months a lighthouse was erected in December 1806. It proved an instant benefit because during the following ten years not a single vessel foundered there.

Hull, because of its burgeoning trade, had the largest complement of Customs officers, mainly based in the port itself, though there were other officers at York, Selby, Gainsborough, Barton and Patrington (near Spurn Head). There was always a small Revenue vessel stationed at the port to patrol the estuary and the Lincolnshire and Holderness coasts. Most of the bigger and better armed Revenue cutters that battled with the large smuggling luggers and the French and Dutch privateers were based at Newcastle and controlled by the collector there, much to the annoyance of the Yorkshire collectors, who felt with some justification that they were in the best position to direct their operations. The Customs records of the area are full of pleas for a strong maritime presence along the coast as the only real solution to 'this pernicious and infamous trade'. However, as we will see later, the many clashes with smuggling vessels at sea tended to be very one-sided affairs and did little to staunch the flow of smuggled goods.

Considering the state and extent of smuggling along the Yorkshire coast, the Customs forces devoted solely to its control and prevention were sadly inadequate. The riding officers, in the forefront of the battle against smuggling, were woefully outnumbered. Until the early years of the 19th century no more than 20 such officers covered the whole stretch of the Yorkshire coast, and they well merit the description 'the thin blue line'.

These officers were compelled to live and work in very hostile communities that wholeheartedly supported and assisted the trade. They faced overwhelming odds, were frequently intimidated, suffered violence and at times were censured by their superiors for lack of urgency and vigilance because of the dearth of seizures.

As if such factors and conditions were not sufficient to fully test and tax the Customs men, they had other problems to contend with. The rugged nature of the coast and the sheer number of landing places made their work even more difficult. The riding officers were strangers to the area they served, a deliberate policy to prevent collusion with relatives or friends who may have been involved in the free-trade. The smugglers, on the other hand, were born and bred in the area and knew every natural feature of the coast intimately and they used their local knowledge to great advantage.

Furthermore the abysmal state of the roads in the county made movement difficult, especially in the winter. For instance in Holderness it was said that 'at this time of the year [December] the ways are next to impossible, and some have lost their lives who have ventured through them'. A journey from Whitby to Hull could take as long as five days' hard riding even without any added problems of flooded rivers or snow. Even as late as 1830 the Whitby collector took two whole days to go to Guisborough and return – a distance of 21 miles. The parlous state of communication made the movements of troops from either Beverley or York to the troubled parts of the coast a rather slow and ponderous business. The riding officer at Marske reported in January 1743 that he had been unable 'to attend my ride for the trechorous[sic] snow falls that has made passage impossible . . .', though despite the weather conditions he had heard that '. . . some runs was made on the coast nearby . . .'. This letter did not arrive at the Stockton Custom House until ten days later – a distance of only 15 miles! In January 1792, Simon Collier was moved from Hull to become riding officer at Marske and he took eleven days to travel the 104 miles.

Most Customs officers in other areas of the country relied on receiving information of impending smuggling runs. Despite the punishment meted out to informers should they be discovered, the rewards offered by the Customs were sufficiently attractive to encourage some brave individuals to take the risk. However, in 49

Yorkshire there is hardly any evidence at all of the receipt of information. This situation may be explained by the fact that all the fishing villages were closed communities with considerable intermarriage, thus maintaining a solid and uncommunicative front to all outsiders.

Thus the scenario for Yorkshire smuggling. It was not until the formation of the Preventive Waterguard in 1809 that the balance of power was, at long last, tipped in favour of the Customs. Within a couple of years the number of Customs officers solely employed for the prevention of smuggling had increased quite dramatically. Preventive boats were provided at Coatham, Staithes, Robin Hood's Bay, Scarborough, Filey, Bridlington and Hull. Then with the arrival of the Coastguard in 1823 the numbers of Revenue officers along the coast increased until there were no less than 150 men patrolling and guarding the coast, with a strong Revenue presence at sea. The scales were now heavily balanced in the Revenue's favour and they held the upper hand. However, it could be argued that this was almost a case of overkill, or too much, too late. By this time, largely due to a reduction in import duties and changes in smuggling methods, old style smuggling runs were almost past history. But it is this very history that provides such a rich and fascinating story.

3

Coatham to Staithes:
'A nasty bleak cold place'

In the days before its commercial and industrial development no coastline in all Yorkshire could have been more remote and isolated than the splendid stretch of golden sands that extend from the mouth of the Tees to the imposing headland of Hunt Cliff. Though only about ten miles in length this 'nasty bleak cold place', as the area was once described, was able to support no less than four small fishing communities – Coatham, Redcar, Marske and Saltburn. This little known north-east corner of Yorkshire was almost a 'hidden and forgotten place'; the Cleveland Hills formed a formidable barrier to the narrow strip of coast and the sad lack of roads made it virtually inaccessible. It was said that each village was quite distinct from the others though close enough in distance – 'each was scarcely known by their neighbour'. Menacing rocks at Coatham and Redcar and strong currents in the bay make the coast dangerous and rather inhospitable and it has taken an ample toll of shipping over the years. For instance during the great storm of 1861 some 50 vessels came to grief on the coast, and the presence of a Victorian mortuary along the coast at Saltburn is evidence of the number of dead bodies washed up along this shore. The very seclusion, its harsh climate and perilous waters had bred a strong-willed and independent people, many fine and hardy seamen and fishermen – perfect qualification for the smuggling trade.

Coatham at the extremity of the Tees estuary was described variously as 'a mean place' and 'a straggle of habitation'. In 1808 it was said to be no more than 'half a street of about seventy houses', where during the winter months the sands encroached right into the village. A mile or so of open green separated Coatham from Redcar and although Redcar also only had a single street, it could at least boast of houses on *both* sides of the street, though when Charles Dickens made an all too brief visit he dismissed it as 'a long cell'. Just a little further to the south stood probably the most complete and compact community of the area – Marske, or Marsh as it was sometimes shown on old maps. The village comprised a cluster of neat cottages, a couple of inns and the parish church. Set back slightly from the foreshore and its tiny haven, Marske nevertheless was still involved in fishing. And then just a mile or so down the coast almost at the point where the sands run out was Saltburn, little more than a couple of lines of cottages which straggled untidily along the beach, with an inn or so and behind them in the gill (wooded ravine) a water-mill, the odd farm and a few limekilns. It was really more a hamlet than a village. John Hall-Stevenson, the rather eccentric squire of Skelton Castle (a few miles inland from Saltburn), has described the area in verse:

'Next fishy Redcar, view Marske's sunny lands,
And sands beyond Pretolus' golden sands;
'Til shelvy Saltburn, cloth'd with seaweed green,
And giant Huntcliff close the pleasing scene.'

It was indeed a coast that eked out a most precarious living from the sea; fishing cobles lined the sands, there was a fairly brisk trade in coal, timber, lime, kelp (seaweed) and a little corn, but the frequent shipwrecks brought some providential bounty and relief from such a harsh and rude existence. When visiting the coast today with its seaside resorts of Redcar and Saltburn and the industry to the north of Coatham you may have difficulty visualising the area as it was in the 18th century. However, salvation came in another bonus from the sea – smuggling. No longer a forgotten corner, all too soon it would be famed as one of the most active smuggling areas along the whole east coast of England. In 1769 the *Newcastle Chronicle* reported that accounts they had received from Redcar and Saltburn suggested that 'smuggling is carried on to a major extent . . . the great number of country people that daily attend the coast (and seem to have no other employ but to carry off the goods) is almost incredible . . .' In 1690 the Customs Board in London were, for once, aware of the dangers of an escalation of smuggling due largely to a vast increase in import duties of all kinds – both Customs and Excise. Many and various trade restrictions and prohibitions were also

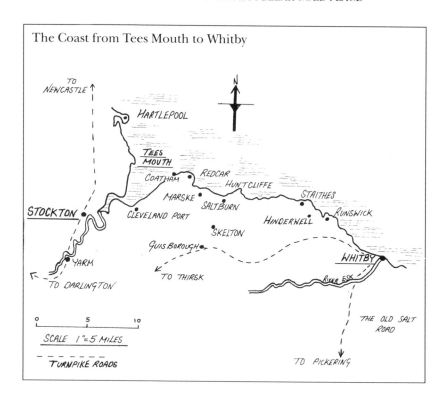

The Coast from Tees Mouth to Whitby

introduced. In February the Customs Board issued an instruction to all the Customs collectors that provides a fitting introduction to the new era of smuggling.

'The late act prohibiting all trade and Commerce with France and Ireland has occasioned great art and Industry to be used in Carrying on the smuggling trade and privattie stealing on shore. Both prohibiting and unCustomed goods to the great hindrance and prejudice of their Majesties Reveniew of Customs . . . you and all the officers of your port are to quicken greater diligence in looking out for the preventing of fraudes of this Kinde and you are all to take Notice that if wee shall hereafter know of any goods Rune with the lymits of your port wee shall account itt as the Neglect of your selves and the other officers and wee will proceede against you . . .'

Strong words and fine sentiments maybe but they were rapidly overtaken by a vast explosion of smuggling in the next century. 53

Not until nine years later did the Customs Board decide to establish a landguard of riding officers along the coast. Each officer received a salary of £90 per year, to include the cost of 'a servant and a horse'. Each was allocated an area of coast to patrol, normally about ten miles in length, and almost tailor-made for the coast from Coatham to Saltburn. So it is not surprising, by the beginning of the new century, that there was a riding officer based at Marske, working from his own house, which was fairly central for his ride. He came under the control of the collector at Whitby – a distance of about 25 miles. The first known officer in the area was James Carr and judging by the number of seizures he made, despite overwhelming odds, he was a most active and diligent officer. The same could not be said for many other riding officers, some were described as 'no more use than a gull on the shore'! Carr did have some support as there was a small Customs coble at Coatham, and though used mainly to visit vessels in the river Tees, its four boatmen could provide a little extra muscle if and when the occasion demanded. At the same time a small Customs sloop was provided at Newcastle with orders to patrol the coast 'from Berwick to the Humber', far too extensive an area to be other than of purely nominal preventive value.

The first *recorded* seizure of smuggled goods by Carr was in November 1721 when he caught a Thomas Garbutt, 'a known rogue', landing five half-ankers of brandy from his coble on the shore at Marske. Carr must have persuaded Garbutt to disclose where he had sold some of the goods because the following morning Carr searched a barn at Brotton, a small village high up on Hunt Cliff, where he found a couple more half-ankers. Garbutt and his accomplice were successfully prosecuted and fined and the brandy was finally sold for £7. It is interesting to note that the Whitby collector, Hamlet Woods, wrote in most concerned terms to the Customs Board hoping that he had completed the various forms correctly as it was the first prosecution of its kind in the port – not a particularly good record to admit!

Saltburn, which was to prove such a thorn in the Customs' side for the next 100 or so years, makes its first entry into the smuggling records when Carr discovered 'a number of persons running brandy on the sands at Saltburn' who quickly departed as he approached (how things would change!) but Carr suspected

The shore at Saltburn with Hunt Cliff in the distance.

that they were led 'by one named Brunt, who does nothing else but meddle in such affaires'. Carr seemed to spend his time dashing about from one part of his territory to another, seizing a variety of goods at Teesmouth, Redcar, Kirkleaton, Skelton and, of course, Saltburn. Some of them were not the usual smuggled commodities, Carr found 'Spanish juice' (liquorice), iron wire, pepper, sugar loaves, arrach (rice spirit), sack (sherry) and 'drugges' including camphor, cardamom and julep. If nothing else it clearly proved that smugglers were very adaptable and anything that could earn a dishonest sovereign would be run. It was very clear that Saltburn, even then, was the most active village in the trade. Angus Macdonald, the coal meter at 'Lingberry Allom works' (at Loftus), who had a wonderful panoramic view of the bay, reported in 1729 'Tis rare but no but see 3 or 4 smugglers at anchor at Saltburn when the wether is right. Many ships can get out of the harbour there.'

In 1729 the area to the north of Hunt Cliff was transferred from Whitby to the collector at Stockton, a much smaller port but then the only one of any consequence in the Tees estuary. Perhaps this change was a result of Hamlet Woods' admission that he had never visited the coast because 'the terrain and paucity of roads makes the journey very long and most onerous, and my business at this port keeps me most occupied'. Certainly Marske was much closer to Stockton and the presence of a boat at Coatham made the area much more accessible to Stockton. I have no doubt that Woods must have breathed a deep sigh of relief to be rid of this most troublesome smuggling spot.

The change was most beneficial to Carr; his son James junior became an officer at Stockton and in 1799 his grandson John became collector there. Indeed such family connections were quite common in both the Customs and Excise services. Carr's new collector, Peter Consett, asked for his summation of the smuggling activities in Carr's area. The report provides a vivid eye-witness account:

> 'This countrie is full of villains, who carry on the evil trade to some great extent. The shore being of firme sandes offer good landings. Foreign sailes are oft seen in the bay and the cobles make met with them . . . Coatham is a mean place, its people take vantage of its nearness to the river. Redcar has several families who make goodly profite from running goods, which all the countrie people give help and succour and carry them away. This village [Marske] is not so deepe in the trade but nearby Saltburn numbers regularly gather to run goods from colliers and privateers at sea, who are insolent in their manner. What is needed is a mann of warr to cruise the coast, which will greatly benefit the publick revenue and stop this iniquitious trade . . .'

Whether Carr was referring to the activities of a well-known smuggling dogger that was causing considerable problems along the coast is not clear. The term 'dogger' is thought to refer to its employment for fishing on the Dogger Bank rather than a specific design. Certainly this dogger had not only been making frequent runs on the coast but had also been supplying the numerous colliers and cobles around the Tees. Even the name of the vessel was known – the *Young Daniel*, and her master, William Reddouch, was a well-known smuggling figure along the coast.

The Revenue sloop that operated from Newcastle, the *Prince of Wales*, had spent many fruitless months searching for this vessel. Its commander, Captain John Bowen, had been particularly successful in recent years; in 1733 he had seized over 2,000 gallons of brandy, a fair quantity of tea, two small fishing vessels and

56

Revenue vessel similar to the ones that operated along the Yorkshire coast

even two horses! It was in late January 1734 that Bowen sighted the smuggling dogger about 'two miles south of Teesmouth' just off Redcar. As soon as Reddouch saw the *Prince of Wales* bearing down upon him, he hoisted his sails and according to Bowen's report '. . . used every endeavours to cheat us out of the wind, which obliged us to jibe our sales seven times . . .' After a chase which lasted well over seven hours the *Prince of Wales* managed to draw alongside, a small party boarded the dogger and a fierce fight ensued. Reddouch had certainly not given up as the vessel's sails were still set (the lowering of sails was an accepted signal of surrender). After about an hour the vessel was taken but not without injuries on both sides. However, when it was brought into   57

Newcastle there was only a small quantity of brandy on board, most of the cargo had already been landed on the Yorkshire coast.

One of the occupational hazards of a Revenue officer's job is exemplified by the experience of William Saville, the mate of the *Prince of Wales*. Two years after this incident he was committed to Durham Gaol accused of the murder of a smuggler. Although he was ultimately found not guilty, he was confined in prison for well over six months. To add insult to injury, the £5 he had been granted for subsistence whilst in prison was deducted from his salary on his return to duty. Saville served with some distinction on several Revenue vessels on the east coast before retiring from the service at the age of 66 years.

The Excise is first seen entering the smuggling scene in September 1735. Two officers were 'on their ride' – each officer had a set number of parishes to control called 'rides' – near Ormesby, just about five miles inland from Marske. They decided to challenge a heavily loaded farm cart that was trundling towards them. Whereupon 'the two waggoners leaped off and ran across the fields before we could stop them'. Under a pile of potatoes they uncovered eleven half-ankers of brandy, six of geneva, 20 pounds of tea and some striped cambric. The officers commandeered an outhouse at a nearby inn and deposited the seized goods under a crown lock until they could make suitable arrangements for their transfer to Stockton. During the night several attempts were made to rescue the goods but they were fought off with the help of the innkeeper.

Just two years later there is a very rare instance of a collector becoming actively involved in the day-to-day work of his officers. They normally sat tight in their Custom Houses and exhorted their staff to greater energy and vigilance from the safety of their warm and comfortable offices. James Carr and his collector called at the house of Smithies near Marske, who was the agent of the Lord of the Manor, the Dundas family. They were concerned about a quantity of goods said to have been salvaged from the wrecked vessel *Gripple*, which had come ashore near Redcar. The Customs had the responsibility of securing salvaged goods and charging duty on them. However, under ancient wreck laws the Lord of the Manor could rightfully claim ownership providing they were genuinely salvaged and not smuggled goods that had been washed ashore.

Smithies had 'absented himselfe and could not be met...', perhaps he had a guilty conscience. His wife was questioned 'in a most civil manner' but she proved to be most obtuse and refused to tell them where the goods were and said 'she would report us to her Lord'. They could not get any information from 'the rest of the inhabitants they greeted us with blanke stares...' So the collector was left with no alternative but 'to write to Hon. Commissioners to enquire of the Lord of the Manor'. This was a prime example of the problems that beset the Customs along the Yorkshire coast over wrecked goods.

The ubiquitous Carr almost seemed to have been fighting a single-handed battle against smuggling in his area. His seizures came from every part of the coast – brandy at Coatham, geneva at Redcar, tea and tobacco at Marske, and playing cards and tobacco at Yerby, just a few miles inland. But perhaps his best haul occurred in 1737 when he and several officers (maybe the Coatham boatmen) seized 25 half-ankers of brandy, 30 pounds of tobacco and a large quantity of tea from a coble at Saltburn. Although they encountered strong opposition 'from a gathering of countrie people' they still managed to secure the goods. As he reported to the collector, '...such insolent and rude behaviour should not go unpunished as it may grow into an ill...'! It was probably just as well that Carr had left the scene before the brutality of the trade escalated over the next 50 years.

This apparent increase in the use of force by the smugglers might be a direct response to the Smugglers Act of 1736, which really can be seen as a declaration of war upon them. This act imposed the death penalty on smugglers using arms, and transportation, flogging or hard labour for those resisting arrest. There were also severe penalties for gathering in gangs. But most of the smuggling acts also allowed the imposition of compromise penalties at the Customs own discretion and for most of the first half of the 18th century the Customs seemed rather loath to prosecute the routine small-time smuggler. It was considered preferable to seize the goods and vessel, which would reward the officers and also cause real distress to the smugglers. However, when the smugglers gathered in sizeable and well-armed gangs and opposed the Revenue with force, it became a vastly different and, at times, deadly matter.

Judging by the number of seizures recorded at Stockton for the period 1740 to 1755 the amount of smuggling seems to have abated quite considerably. This, of course, is a dangerous assumption to make as the absence of seizures does not necessarily indicate a reduction in the trade; it could also mean that the smugglers were becoming more successful and that they were opposed by less urgent and zealous Customs officers. Indeed during this period James Carr retired and was replaced by a Richard Vickerman, who hardly ever figures in the Customs records. Nevertheless a decline in smuggling during this period does equate with the situation elsewhere in the country. This charge may be somewhat attributed to a reduction in import duties, especially tea and tobacco, and the greater and more successful use of troops against the smugglers. Then, with the outbreak of the Seven Years War in 1756, duties increased sharply and there were few troops available to assist the Revenue with the result that the smuggling trade flared back into life. This is borne out by the plaintive request, in December 1756, from William Kilner, the Customs Surveyor at Stockton:

'. . . the need for some good extraordinary [not on the complement] men till some other provision is made . One or more smugglers were off the coast about 3 weeks or a month. They run their cargoes on York coast opposite us [between Newport and Coatham] and on the North York sands. We have besides at least 7 or 8 miles of the coast to guard and cobles can land anywhere where the sea is smooth, for when we go along the Coast at night there must be 2 or 3 together otherwise they hazard their lifes and without being able to secure the run goods. The cobles 2 to 3 hands with often above a dozen Country men with horses to carry them off. It is our informacion that the trade is increased of late . . .'

Not a single extra man was recruited and there is no evidence that the collector even bothered to apply to the Customs Board in London for any increase in staff. Perhaps one of the reasons for this lack of enthusiasm was that seven years later the collector, John Watson, was dismissed from his post over 'irregularities in his accounts . . . [he had] acted in concert with some merchants to the injury of the Public Revenue'. A hint that perhaps he was also in league with the smuggling fraternity? Nevertheless in 1771 he was appointed Mayor of Hartlepool.

60   Kilner's appreciation of the vulnerability of the Tees coast and

his concern at the ease with which it was used in the trade was fully justified in April 1759. Richard Sansom, an Excise officer and his servant were waiting to cross the river by ferry when they saw four men gaily landing goods near 'Cleaveland Port [now Middlesborough] from a river coble at after 2 in the afternoon'. Sansom identified himself and 'a sharp exchange of blows took place'. One of the smugglers was shot in the arm and 'Mr Watt, my servant, received some harsh blows to his head and shoulders but bravely assisted me.' The two Excise men stood their ground doggedly and managed to secure the goods – eight half-ankers of geneva, 46 pounds of tea, three rolls of tobacco, two canisters of coffee and seven bricks of soap (there was a high Excise duty on soap). Three of the smugglers made their escape, leaving just Joseph Merryman to face the music. It was said that he was 'a fisherman from Redcar and known to be in the trade'. The coble was seized and later destroyed by burning. Merryman was ultimately convicted, fined £40 and like many other convicted smugglers ended up in Durham gaol as a Crown debtor unable to find such a substantial sum – possibly three times the annual wage of a labourer.

John Davidson, the newly appointed Stockton collector, quickly showed he was a different character to his predecessor. He literally bombarded London with dire reports of the extent of smuggling in his area, as well as many requests for extra staff. In 1767 he even put forward a strong case for 'a small cutter' to be established at Stockton. He maintained that it should be 'very fast, well manned and commanded by a diligent and experienced officer to cruise between Hartlepoole and Whitby'. In his opinion 'such a vessel properly managed with the assistance of the gentlemen of the country and our valiant officers would greatly reduce the iniquitous practice of smuggling on the Yorkshire coast'. A rather optimistic and somewhat naive assessment of the situation, especially as most country gentlemen condoned the trade and were eager recipients of smuggled brandy, wines and tea. Davidson also mentioned that when his Surveyor and the tidesmen were relieved of their other duties (dealing with legal trade vessels), 'they had gone upon the Yorkshire coast and have lately made some considerable seizures'. He was referring to a couple of seizures made at Marske and Redcar of tea, brandy and geneva to a value of £325. On each occasion no culprits were caught and some of the goods had been discovered hidden in the sand dunes.

Just a year later, in April, he felt it necessary to inform London that 'the smuggling on the Yorkshire coast is carried on in a most flagrant manner with no less than four cutters laden with contraband goods having lately been seen cruising off the coast ... Every step has been taken by our officers to put a stop to this pernicious practice and a pretty considerable seizure has been made lately in this port from one of the cobles that plies between the smuggling vessels and the shore ...' He then went on to condemn the Customs commanders of vessels in most direct and vehement terms '. . . their indolence and inactivity is well-known . . . they do not communicate or contact the coast officers . . . they are of so little use that the smuggling vessels run very little hazard of being taken . . .' Certainly those operating from Newcastle had gained precious little success. The Customs Board passed the criticism on to the Newcastle collector – Langdale Sunderland. He made it quite clear that he had 'the utmost confidence in my Commanders' but he explained that 'they were opposed by such large well-armed luggers that cannot be matched by our small cutters'. He suggested that Davidson was 'green to the business and with longer experience he will fully understand this infernal smuggling trade'!

The 'pretty considerable seizure' was probably the haul made at Saltburn in January 1768. A party of six Customs men in their small coble watched patiently as goods were being landed at Saltburn from a large coble. When they considered that the time was right, they moved inshore and challenged the landing party. The smugglers were quite prepared to defend their goods and 'armed with heavy bats they attacked with vigour . . .' However, several pistol shots from the Customs 'dispersed the country people'. The smugglers were thought to have 'come from Skelton' and there was a man named Hutton at that village who was known to be in the smuggling trade, especially in tobacco. The seized goods – geneva, tea, tobacco – were taken to Marske (probably the house of the riding officer) where they were guarded overnight until they could be taken to the King's warehouse at Stockton.

The increasing violence in the area was most disquieting for the Customs. In October 1774 Walter Parks, the riding officer at

Marske, received some serious injuries when he attempted to prevent a landing of goods at Redcar. The surgeon who attended him and was paid five guineas for his professional services, wrote of 'the great many contusions from being violently beaten by certain smugglers, particularly of your right arm and shoulder, which threatened mortification . . . the hard tumour in your shoulder endangered the use of the arm and hand thereon . . .' Parks recovered and the Customs Board finally reimbursed him for the cost of the treatment but at this time there were no compensation payments for injuries sustained during the course of their duties.

With fearful apprehension that the smuggling situation was getting very seriously out of hand, the collector pressed London for troops 'to assist my beleagured officers who face violence daily . . .' It took another two urgent requests before he was informed in December 1774 that orders had been given to 'the Officer in command of the Royal North British dragoons at York to render assistance to the Customs at Stockton'. A sergeant, corporal and 18 men arrived in the area on Christmas Eve and were placed at Coatham, Redcar and Marske.

The troops were normally billeted at local inns and their presence was certainly not welcome. In those days soldiers were considered 'outsiders', in fact they themselves felt they 'were not of the people'. As a general policy regiments were frequently moved around the country, permanent barracks were rare and the troops were well used to being billeted in inns, where as the allowance given to innkeepers for their keep was meagre, they were allocated very inferior accommodation and given very poor food. When on smuggling duties the troops were awarded an extra 2d a day and promised a proportion of the seizure rewards, but one of the problems was that the processing of seizure money took an inordinate time and often they didn't see the extra money for many months if at all, if they were serving abroad when the smuggling case was finally settled. All this meant that they were less than urgent in their smuggling duties. The efficacy of the dragoons in preventing smuggling has been greatly exaggerated. All their training was in formal warfare so they were not really suited to deal with the guerilla tactics of the smugglers. Indeed there is little evidence of many seizures of consequence that were made by the military when they were in the area.

In April 1775 Davidson's perseverance paid off when the Customs Board agreed that a smuggling coble captured near Hartlepool could be taken into the Revenue service. It was renamed the *Ferret* and they accepted a Captain Major as its contractor and commander. At that time there were two different methods of employment of Revenue vessels. The first was a properly established vessel – owned and fully operated by the Crown. The alternative was a contract vessel, where although it was owned by the Crown no hiring charge was made to the contractor but he was responsible for its repair and maintenance including the crew's wages, which were paid directly out of the seizure rewards and then any residue was shared equally between the Crown and the contractor. It was under this latter method that the *Ferret* was employed at Stockton.

Poor Davidson must have rued the day that Captain Major walked into his Custom House; he caused endless trouble and indeed was nothing more than a walking disaster! Major had been appointed to command a Revenue cutter at Southampton in April 1769. He not only wrecked the vessel off the Guernsey coast but got himself imprisoned for seizing two legally trading vessels. After great difficulty the Customs Board managed to extricate him from prison and offered him another command as a form of recompense. Major managed to wreck this vessel off the Isle of Wight; to lose one vessel might be considered bad luck; losing two might be thought a trifle careless! Major so badgered the Customs Board with letters that they finally offered him the *Ferret* mainly to get shot of him.

Within months of his arrival Major was complaining of lack of cash to provide food for the vessel and the collector was forced to send him £10 to tide him over. In December 1775, he and his vessel made its one and only seizure of smuggled goods. It captured a small smuggling cutter off the coast near Saltburn. The Revenue crew moved the spirits, tobacco and sails from the cutter but the following day Major visited the smuggling vessel again, this time on his own. According to Thomas Dykes, the long-suffering mate of the *Ferret*, Major clubbed the smuggling master around the head with his pistols and then took him below to negotiate an agreement with the smugglers – a share of their profits provided he agreed not to interfere with their activities! Accusations and counter-accusations flowed freely, the crew had not been paid any salary and Major refused to part with any of the £104 he had received in reward money. By March 1776 half of his crew had deserted and soon the rest followed suit. Major wrote to the Customs Board in September complaining of 'his great sufferings and anxiety . . . running through my small fortune and spending that which should provide for my children at my decease . . .' He got no response and by November reported that there were so many rats on board his vessel that 'they would soon be eating the sails'! The vessel stayed in port, falling into a sad state of disrepair and Major's contract was not formally ratified. The end of the sorry story came in April 1779 when Major was dismissed from the Customs service for sending a letter threatening the life of Sir William Musgrave, a Customs Commissioner, and one of the most able administrators of the 18th century.

As a counterbalance to the attitude and character of officers like Major, one has the unsung heroes of the Customs service – those who lived and worked in such a hostile corner of Yorkshire. The day-to-day work of such stalwart officers was beset with frustration, intimidation and the threat of violence. John Ferry, the riding officer at Coatham, was one such officer who tried conscientiously to carry out his orders. One December morning in 1775 he found a rather nasty threatening letter left on his doorstep:

'Damn you Damn you Ferry and Parks blast you Ise [eyes] you say that you will Exchequer all Redcar but if you do damn my Ise if we don't smash your Brains out. You may as well take what we give you as other officers do and if you dont well sware that you take bribes you had better take them to encourage you. What did giv Parks for his basting [October 1774] that Nicholls People gave them. Damn your Ise keep off the sands or else.'

The collector passed the letter on to London with a covering report praising both Ferry and Parks as 'brave and most diligent officers, who work tirelessly for the Public Revenue . . .' and faithfully stated that he would make his own investigations into the hints of bribery. However, like many similar inquiries held in other ports no positive result was achieved and there were certainly no records of any dismissals at Stockton during this period.

In August 1778 Walter Parks had heard of some geneva being washed ashore at Marske. The eight casks (32 gallons) had been quickly claimed by Smithies, the agent of Sir Laurence Dundas, the Lord of the Manor. However, this time Parks managed to gain an interview with the old man – he must have been in his eighties – and persuaded him that they should be secured under joint locks until the true ownership was established. Parks reported that his information 'supposed that the said casks had been anchored at sea by the crew of a smuggling vessel and having broken loose were drive ashore and therefore belong to the Crown but he [Smithies] would not hear of such a thing . . .' Unfortunately the outcome of this dispute is not known.

This incident highlights one of the most popular stratagems used by smugglers. The idea was to sink spirit tubs close to the shore attached to a recovery line, which was normally marked by a small buoy. The goods could then be recovered at an appropriate time. This operation was known in smuggling parlance as 'sowing the crop'. In an attempt to counter the ploy, one of the regular duties of the Revenue boats was to patrol the shore using grappling irons in the hope of locating such sunken goods. This activity was known as 'creeping' and was most unpopular with the crew as it was very time-consuming, tedious and largely unproductive. Perhaps the most interesting aspect of the report is that it is the earliest reference to this smuggling method being used anywhere in the country. Hitherto it had been assumed that such a ploy did not come into general use until the 1820s, when it was used fairly frequently and most effectively, especially along the south coast of England.

The *Newcastle Courant* of 19th February 1780 has a report of a rather hectic Sunday morning:

'Last Sunday as the people were going from Coatham to Kirleatham church they were alarmed by the fire of a large gun from a smuggler at sea, which carried 24 guns, 9 and 12 pounders. The people saw about 70 or 80 of the crew coming from the ship in long boats, armed with blunderbusses, pistols etc, in order to rescue a large seizure of liquors made at Redcar by the Whitby officers, attended by four of the Cumberland Militia. As soon as the smugglers landed they retook part of the seizure at Redcar and Coatham, and staved in the heads for the populace to drink and pursing the carts etc. laden with the other part, they came up with them near Wilton [about two miles south-west of

COATHAM TO STAITHES: 'A NASTY BLEAK COLD PLACE'

The 'Old Ship Inn' Saltburn – haunt of John Andrew – and now a smuggling museum.

Kirkleatham], and seized the remainder, the officers and soldiers having expended all their rounds, but happily no lives were lost. They then staved three casks there, one in Wilton wood, and carried the remainder back.'

Unfortunately there is no reference to this incident either in the Whitby or Stockton Customs records. However, one wonders if the infamous John Andrew was either involved or perhaps witnessed the whole affair?

John Andrew has been dubbed 'The King of the Smugglers', a title that was rumoured to have been bestowed upon him by his daughter. He certainly became a folk hero par excellence along this area of the coast and his old Ship Inn has now been converted into a smuggling museum – The Saltburn Smugglers – largely devoted to his memory and escapades. Amongst all the countless smuggling legends surrounding him, one fact is very clear, there is not a single reference to him in the Customs records of the period; but perhaps this just testifies to his very success at the trade, always suspected but never caught, at least until the very end of his career.

What is known of John Andrew? He was born into a Scottish farming family and brought up in the Montrose area, which was 67 not only noted for its strong Jacobite affiliations but also as a notorious smuggling spot. Such a background would suggest that the young Andrew would readily enter the smuggling trade at Saltburn. The Customs and Excise services were even more hated in Scotland than in England, if indeed that was possible! I am sure that Andrew would have felt a touch of satisfaction in evading the hated Hanoverian taxes. Apparently he arrived in the area in 1778, certainly he married a local girl from Skelton in 1780. He soon settled in as the landlord of the Ship Inn, which was situated right on the shore at Saltburn and, by repute, entered the smuggling trade with great gusto. As already mentioned this hamlet had long been deeply involved in the free-trade. The inn with its magnificent position on the sands would have made a splendid centre for operations and thus any landlord would have been considered a prime suspect by the Revenue.

What must be remembered is that all inns were regularly visited by Excise officers during their normal course of duty. This was not only to check stocks of spirits and wines but also to calculate the Excise duty on the beer brewed by the publican – in those days most publicans brewed their own beer. No spirits or wines could be moved throughout the country without an official permit signed by an Excise officer to prove that they were duty-paid. The permit system had been introduced in the early decades of the 18th century in an attempt to control the movement of goods. In theory all spirits being conveyed without an Excise permit were automatically considered to be smuggled and the same applied to goods found in the publican's stock. With the frequency of Excise visits, especially as the officers had the legal right to search all parts of the premises including the living quarters, the use of inns for the storage of smuggled goods was a most hazardous business indeed. Most so-called smuggling inns were more likely just to have been used by smugglers as a rendezvous – a place where they could plan and arrange their next run without too much attention being drawn to them.

Andrew is said to have joined forces with a Thomas King, a brewer of Kirkleatham, who was then thought to be the leader of the smuggling in the area. Certainly there was a family connection, Andrew's daughter later married King. Reputedly after some early successes the two men invested in a lugger called *Morgan Butler*, which legally traded out of Stockton but used

Flushing as its base for smuggled goods. The master of the vessel, Captain Brown, had a reputation as a fine and fearless sailor not averse to using violence in the pursuit of his trade.

In 1804 Andrew was commissioned as an ensign in the Third regiment of the Cleveland Volunteer Infantry and in less than five years was made a captain in the local militia. Considering that on occasions the local militia were called out to support the Customs, the situation in North Yorkshire might have been thought a trifle ludicrous with one of the officers a known smuggler – it would have done justice to Gilbert and Sullivan! However, Andrew prospered and his profits from the smuggling trade enabled him to purchase an imposing farmhouse, known as The White House, set high upon the cliffs overlooking Saltburn and said to be the centre of his smuggling organisation with the cellars used to store smuggled goods. One local historian has written '. . . in the last stall of the old stables . . . on the seaward side, was a false floor which gave access to the cellars in which the Free-Traders stored their barrels of duty-free rum and gin from Holland. When the preventive men searched the premises, they [some of Andrew's gang] put in that stall a mare which they could trust to kick viciously at any stranger'!

By 1817 Andrew had been appointed Master of Fox Hounds to the Cleveland Hunt. He had now become the epitome of a country gentleman of his time, he had managed to climb up the social ladder and was fully accepted by the local gentry. It was even said that he supplied a large part of the wedding trousseau of the daughter of the first Lord Dundas, whose seat was at Marske Hall. These were the days when there was a complete trade embargo on all French goods and John Andrew supplied many of those luxuries of life – brandy, wines, silks, lace and gloves – that ultimately found their way into the households of his fellow hunt members. John Andrew demonstrated just how profitable the smuggling trade could be and he was certainly one of the very few smugglers who managed to take the huge step to become a 'gentleman' as well.

Whilst the fight against the smugglers on land continued unabated and with increasing ferocity, the battle, if that is the correct term, at sea was a vastly different affair. Some of the Customs commanders were quite successful, whereas others appeared to operate like privateers rather than Revenue officers 69 and some were grossly incompetent and out-and-out rogues (after the style of James Major). Most of them seemed to have scant regard for any kind of officialdom or discipline either in the guise of the Customs Board or closer to home – the collectors at the ports. Almost all of them played the game to their own rules and manipulated the system to suit themselves. There were dark hints that some were in league with the smugglers, often seizing small cargoes just for effect, whilst conniving with the landing of much larger cargoes. Certainly every area of the coast and almost every port could boast their own special characters.

One commander who could be fairly described as such a character was Captain Thomas Armstrong, who operated off the Yorkshire coast from his home port of Newcastle. From 1760 onwards for about 30 years he commanded the *Bridlington, Charlotte* and *Mermaid,* sometimes with certain flair, on very odd occasions with bravery but for most of the time with a conspicuous lack of success. It was strongly rumoured that he was in league with the smugglers and, although he was suspended from duty on at least two occasions whilst his activities were closely investigated, he managed to survive and retire from the service without a stain on his character. Armstrong had a strong family backing in New-castle: one brother, Nicholas, was the supervisor of the riding officers, another brother, Robert, was the mate of the *Eagle* (the second vessel stationed in the port) and his cousin Richard was the collector's clerk – nepotism run riot!

In December 1774 the *Mermaid* was anchored just about a mile or so off Saltburn when a large smuggling shallop appeared and its master insisted that Armstrong 'took up the anchor and departed lest he blow us out of the water . . .' Armstrong meekly complied with this order and left the bay without even a token show of resistance. Armstrong's excuse was that he could see another large smuggling vessel bearing down upon him and felt '. . . so inferior in force and not able to cope, nor should I hazard my vessel in such circumstances . . .' The large smuggling vessel was identified as the *Porcupine,* which was about 130 tons with a crew of not less than 40 and was armed with 14 carriage guns, four three-pounders and a great number of swivel guns. It was commanded by David Browning, who was nick-named 'Smoker'. Browning's brother, Edward, was the mate and another brother, George, operated on shore – he collected the orders and the money. It was said that he managed this side because he was the only one who could read and write! The three brothers formed a most formidable smuggling firm. They were highly successful and the very name Browning struck terror all along the Yorkshire coast.

Just three years later Captain Whitehead of the *Eagle* gave chase to a smuggling vessel about three miles off Saltburn. When the two vessels closed Whitehead challenged the vessel to hove to, whereupon Browning (Whitehead said he recognised his voice) '. . . used some horrid expressions and immediately discharged up to 30 muskets and several of the swivels wounding several of my men . . .' With this sudden attack the majority of the Revenue seamen 'quitted the deck in fear of their lives, so I considered it prudent to retire . . .' The *Eagle* was chased and harried for the best part of an hour, and finally arrived back to the safety of Newcastle with '20 shots in her sails, a dozen or so in the boats, some of the main mast and mizzen halyards shot away.' Considering that the *Eagle* was then the largest Revenue vessel afloat with no less than twelve carriage guns, it does not say much for either the seamanship of Whitehead or the determination and bravery of the crew.

In March 1779 the *Mermaid* was involved in a rather strange incident off Saltburn. The vessel was engaged in a fight with a lugger that was busily landing a cargo of geneva. Attracted by the sound of gunfire Walter Parks and John Ferry watched the fight from the shore. They started to make plans to seize and transport away some 200 half-ankers, which had already been landed on the beach. However, they were quite shocked to see another boat pull away from the smuggling vessel and '15 strong armed men came ashore and rescued the goods that we could do nothing to prevent it . . .' The two Customs men had to stand helplessly by whilst the goods were reloaded into the boat and moved further along the shore. Frustrated at losing such a valuable seizure the two men then witnessed a quantity of goods being transferred to the *Mermaid* before it sailed away leaving the smuggling vessel to carry on landing the remainder of its cargo. To the two men it seemed a blatant case of connivance. Parks sent an indignant report to his collector at Stockton, which ultimately arrived in Newcastle and Captain Armstrong was asked to explain his actions. His reply was curt and to the point: 'I was not on board at 71 the time, my mate Mr Bland was in command'. No suggestion of any concern for the apparent unusual circumstances. Richard Bland's explanation has not survived but he certainly remained in the Customs service and just a few years later was appointed the commander of a new cutter based at Yarmouth in East Anglia.

In March 1780, the Stockton collector summed up the state of smuggling along the coast and it made rather disheartening reading . . .

'. . . it has of late been carried on to a very great height upon the Yorkshire coast. There having been not less than 3 or 4 smuggling vessels at anchor for near a fortnight past who have run a considerable quantity of geneva, tea and other goods without having received the least molestation from any of the King's or Custom House cutters . . . these goods are landed in complete defiance of the officers and the country people are constantly in waiting and being armed with bludgeons etc and provided with horses, immediately convey the goods to some distant places and their numbers being generally considerable so that the officers are quite unable to cope with them, their position is dire . . .'

What happened in Coatham in December 1783 could not be considered an isolated incident. John Ferry became aware of a large landing on the night of the 12th, so the following morning he and two boatmen searched the village, where they found three casks of geneva, two bags of raw coffee and three bags of tea in a farmyard. They took the goods directly to the house of John Agar, a local magistrate at Coatham, for security. As they left the house they were faced by 'forty upwards of the inhabitants', who proceeded to attack them with '. . . sticks, brickbats and stones . . .' One of the Customs men was so badly beaten that it was thought that he might lose the sight of his left eye. They retreated 'to the house of Mr Johnson, innkeeper' pursued by the mob and '. . . begged for his assistance and the mob attacked the house with great fury, broke several windows and did much damage to his house . . .' It was not until Agar appeared that '. . . the mob was calmed and we were able to make our escape . . .'

Matters certainly did not improve at Coatham because, one November night seven years later, Ferry, together with two boatmen were patrolling the sands when they came across a group of coblemen unloading some ankers of brandy. The three men were held while the goods were loaded onto horses and were warned 'we'll split your sculls if you try to take our goods'. However, quite undaunted by their experience of the previous evening, the following morning they searched the sand dunes and uncovered eleven half-ankers of geneva and brandy. This time they did not waste any time in getting the seized goods down the river to the Customs warehouse at Stockton. Somewhat sad to relate John Ferry died in harness aged 52 years. No doubt his early death was in some part due to working long hours in all weathers and to the physical violence he had suffered during his career.

From Saltburn Beck the character of the coast changes quite dramatically; it rises sharply to the heights of Hunt Cliff, Boulby and Beacon Hill to provide some of the most spectacular scenery along the whole of the east coast of England. In 1974 it was quite rightly designated a Heritage Coast from Saltburn to Scalby Ness near Scarborough. It now forms part of the Cleveland Way, just one of the many national trails in England and Wales. This part of the Way can be closely followed the 50 or so miles to Filey. Along this quite splendid route are ample reminders of its days of the free-trade; smuggling villages, various inns which claim links with the trade, smugglers' caves and look-outs, brandy paths, and old Coastguard paths and cottages. All these suggest that a most active illegal trade was conducted along the whole stretch of this coast for much of the 18th and early 19th centuries.

The rugged nature of the coast along to Sandsend, with its quite magnificent but awesome cliffs rising sheer from a turbulent sea, afforded few opportunities for the smuggling trade. It was only where nature provided some respite from the precipitous terrain with small, narrow and sheltered wykes that the free-trade was able to prosper. The fishing communities of Skinningrove, Staithes and Runswick Bay all became involved in smuggling. The cliff-top villages of Lofthouse (Loftus), Easington and Hinderwell played their part in the distribution of the smuggled goods into the wild and secretive moorland.

Skinningrove is blessed with a sandy beach (Cathersby Sands), well known as a landing place for smuggled goods even in the 1720s. The Whitby collector vouchsafed the view that 'at Skinningrove goods are landed at this place but not in such quantities as to concern the Publick Revenue . . .'. In February 73

1722 Angus Macdonald, the alum officer at Lingberry, seized five half-ankers of brandy at the village but he said he was unable to identify the culprit as 'he escaped into the inn'. Just a year later when he stopped three men on the road out of the village, they had four half-ankers of brandy and 40 pounds of Bohea tea and 20 pounds of green tea. Bohea was the favourite with smugglers as it was largely used by the working classes, green tea was of a better quality and thus slightly more expensive. The three men 'threw the goods away and rode away, 'tis thought that they come from York'. A couple of months later Macdonald found just one half-anker of brandy at 'the house of Emma Huntriss, a poor widow of this place [Skinningrove]'. It is not clear what happened to the 'poor widow' but at the worst she would have been fined. Even James Carr, the riding officer from Marske, managed to get into the act with seizures of brandy and geneva 'on the shore from a coble of Milburn, who made his escape with the help of the people of the dissolute place'! It is quite easy to visualise Carr surrounded by an angry crowd of villagers strongly objecting to his interference in their affairs. I think they had little trouble from Macdonald, their local officer, because according to the Whitby collector he was often the worse for drink:

'Last Saturday I [the collector] received a letter of complaint from Mr More that you was not sober for two days together when upon duty as there is several masters of ships will give their affidavits for. I advise you as a friend to keep yourself compass when you are delivering Coal Ships, for if you don't you may find ill ye consequences thereof, for I doubt not there are people waiting for to take all advantages so I think it behoveth you well as other officers to be on their guard as much as they can possibly . . . I have heard likewise that you expressed yourself in the same manner last Sunday by falling off ye squab [chair] . . .'

Perhaps Macdonald's drinking habits explain why the Excise had far greater success in the area than the Customs. During the 1730s there was a most alert and active Excise officer stationed at Lofthouse – Charles Michael. He made a succession of seizures of brandy, tea and geneva in and around Lofthouse and Skinningrove. The goods were mostly found under hedgerows or hidden in a barn and one small consignment of tea (ten pounds) was concealed in a hollow of a stone wall around the church. But

74

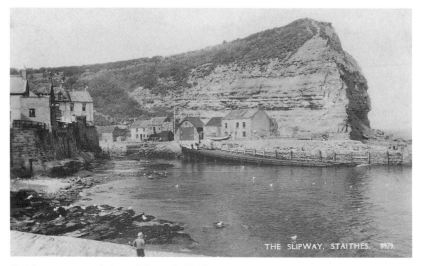

Staithes, a postcard view of the early 1930s.

perhaps the most unusual seizure was made in May 1737 when Michael discovered 'six packs of playing cards and two bricks of soap in the hollow end of a ale tub'! According to Michael's report '. . . the innkeeper says he has no knowledge but I do not trust him as he is known to this Revenue over his payment of Excise . . .' The Excise supervisor at Whitby recommended that 'his lisense be taken for this serious offense . . .' All brewers and brewing victuallers were required to be licensed by the Excise. However, this man lost his goods, was fined £10 but was able to carry on as publican. It is indeed rare to hear of seizures of playing cards, most of the imported packs came from France and were expensive even without the Customs duty and a separate Excise duty of 6d per pack. For most of the time they were truly luxury items.

But it was both Staithes and Runswick Bay that cornered the smuggling market along this craggy stretch of coast. Quaint, charming and picturesque are not too extravagant adjectives to describe these two quite delightful fishing villages. Staithes almost seems to cower beneath its twin headlands with its maze of streets and lanes huddled along each side of the beck (which now forms the county boundary) and then they rise steeply from the small sheltered harbour. It has always been a hard-working fishing 75 community which has forged a robust and a strongly self-reliant spirit. Facing the North Sea the village has managed to survive the various onslaughts and depredations of winter storms – in 1812 nearly one third of the village was washed away. It is steeped in history with links with Captain Cook and the American privateer John Paul Jones, and even today looks just the place where old time smuggling would have abounded. Just about three miles further south lies Runswick Bay with its splendid south facing bay and sands, which attract thousands of summer visitors. This village has also suffered from the ravages of the sea, in 1664 only one house was left standing after a particularly violent storm.

Both villages were notorious in the heyday of smuggling and their success in the trade is best illustrated by the few and rather insubstantial seizures made by either the Customs or Excise. Nevertheless the Whitby collector was well aware of the extent of smuggling in the two villages . . .

> '. . . I am most determined to control these places of the ruinous trade, where it is the opinion of my officers that there is not a single person to be relied upon, even the women are as deep in the trade as their menfolk . . . a recent seizure was only sustained by the use of arms, my officers suffered fearful abuse. I consider that only a body of militia will clear such nests of villains . . .'

As will be shown later even the introduction of the military into the villages failed to bring any order or control to the smuggling scene, and as late as 1817 it was said 'These places, with Robin Hood's Bay, are noted for smuggling. Every friend of mankind will desire the complete suppression of a traffic, so pernicious to the morals of all concerned is it, as to the public revenue and the fair [or legal] trade.'

During the early decades of the 18th century there were a few isolated seizures in and around both villages. In June 1722 Macdonald found a few half-ankers of brandy in 'ye house of Wm. Broderick . . . concealed in a hole in a wall of ye said house'. Indeed it was reported that most of the houses and cottages in Staithes had secret cupboards and hidey holes. Such a situation made it almost impossible for the Customs officers to keep track of landed goods. Contrary to public belief they did not have an inalienable right of access to private houses, they could only demand entry to search if they had strong suspicions or evidence that smuggled goods were being stored or hidden there. They worked with Writs of Assistance, empowering them to search for uncustomed goods. According to the Customs records only 13 half-ankers of brandy and 20 pounds of tea were seized in Staithes in just 18 months and there was even less found in Runswick Bay. Certainly these figures bore no relation to the amount of smuggling carried on.

Another common smuggling myth is that the free-trade was largely concerned with spirits, tobacco and tea. Granted these were the main commodities smuggled, but any article that could show a reasonable return was smuggled, for instance books, candles, dice, sailcloth, salt, soap, and sugar. Candles, an essential part of life for both rich and poor, had an Excise duty of 1d per pound on the tallow kind and 8d per pound on those made from wax, these duties were, of course, in addition to the Customs duties.

But among these items there was always a lively smuggling trade in salt, one of the essentials of life and more especially in fishing communities where considerable quantities were used for the preservation of fish. It was said that as late as 1900 most Yorkshire fisherfolk preferred salt fish to fresh. The old salt road across the moors to Pickering is evidence of the route by which salt came from Cheshire, and the old Saltergate Inn on this most lonely stretch of road had a reputation for smuggled goods. Most of the smuggled salt came from Ireland and Holland. Almost since the inception of the Excise in 1643 salt had been taxed and from 1695 the duty was increased considerably. There were more seizures of salt at Staithes or nearby than anywhere else on the Yorkshire coast, with frequent Excise references to salt being found in farm buildings and wagons and even under hedges. In 1769 an Excise officer found no less than '20 bags of foreign salt weighing 120 lb in an outbuilding of a inn in Staithes'. The name of the inn was not recorded but it could have been the famous Cod and Lobster, right on the quayside. The innkeeper was unable to produce any evidence of duty payment and he was convicted and fined £10. The salt was ultimately auctioned for £12 – worth 2s per pound.

Only in May 1775 did the Whitby collector hear that, at long last, he was to get some military support. Major Horne at York barracks informed him that he had received orders from the War Office to detach one NCO and 16 men to the port. John Burgh

77

The Carronade or "smasher" was introduced to revenue vessels in 1779.

decided to deploy two men at Hinderwell, two at Runswick Bay and four at Staithes. However, far from helping matters their appearance in the area led directly to two fatalities.

The first known confrontation happened in June of the following year. John Hodge, the Runswick officer, along with the two troopers, witnessed a boat coming in to the sands from a large smuggling vessel anchored out in the bay. The boat was well laden with half-ankers of spirits. They immediately moved forward to seize it, at which point they were surrounded by six smugglers who suggested that they were quite prepared to give up the spirits providing their boat was released. They also prevailed upon the troopers '. . . to discharge the pistols to show good faith . . .' One of the number foolishly did so, which seemed to be the signal for a brutal attack. One of the troopers was so severely beaten that he died the following morning. Hodge and the other trooper managed to escape with 'heavy bruises and contusions.' Subsequent enquiries led Hodge to believe that the smugglers belonged to a schooner called *Kent*, which was owned and commanded by a Dover man – George 'Stoney' Fagg. He and his vessel were feared the length and breadth of the Yorkshire coast and had been involved in many engagements with Customs vessels. The *Kent* was well over 160 tons, well armed with 16 four-pounder guns and at least 20 swivels and a crew of upwards of 40 men. The Customs Board offered £100 reward for the capture of the murderers but even such a large monetary incentive did not bring forward any information.

There was a repeat incident at Staithes in the following year when four troopers apprehended a group of local men moving some goods in 'fields above the village'. A sharp interchange of words and insults quickly led to blows. The four soldiers were opposed by a dozen or more smugglers and in the *fracas* Casseldine, one of the troopers, was beaten to the ground and then savagely attacked. Casseldine's face was badly smashed and blood streamed down his uniform. When the local men realised the seriousness of the situation, they withdrew and vanished into the village. Casseldine subsequently died from his injuries.

Charles Spink, the Customs riding officer, recognised one of the attackers from the description given by the troopers – a villager named Richard Curtis. It was said that Curtis had assaulted Casseldine with a heavy bludgeon (possibly part of a ship's mast). Despite the fact that the fight had been watched by many villagers no witnesses could be found – there was a conspiracy of silence. Mr Leonard, a Whitby surgeon who examined Casseldine's body two days after his death, confirmed that there were a great number of bruises with 'blood congealed below his ribs and blows to his head had caused a complete fracture of the left side of his head and eye'. Leonard had no doubt that 'the vicious blows had caused his death'. Curtis was captured and finally brought to trial at the York assizes in July 1779, but the murder charge failed largely because of the surgeon's evidence. According to the collector '. . . Leonard deviated extremely upon the Trayl from what he had before advanced to the Attorney, in consequence whereof Curtis was found not guilty of murder; but on account of the smuggling was suffered by the Judge to enter His Majesty's Sea Service and thus escaped the gallows'.

The Staithes' smugglers seem to have been particularly vicious. Two years later the Whitby collector complained bitterly that the Sheriff's bailiff was having great trouble in trying to serve Writs of Attachment (legal seizures) on two Staithes men accused of 79 smuggling offences – John Wastell and Thomas Crispin. Although the bailiff had spent two days in the village he said 'there is no possibility of taking either man without the assistance of soldiers as they are resolute and always are armed, particularly Wastell, who threatens to shoot the first persons who offer to take him'. Even in February 1781 the collector still thought that they could be taken especially as more troops were to be drafted into the village. But they were never taken, the reason put forward was '. . . being common smugglers and not known where to be found'! But a Mary Newton, said to have been 'a very old woman, maintained by the parish', and 'deep in the trade', was detained for helping Wastell. To arrest a very old woman was not an action to endear the Customs to the villagers and certainly must have brought them a fair amount of ridicule and abuse.

Unfortunately it was the Excise that suffered the backlash of the villagers' anger. In May of the same year an Excise cutter *Lively*, which operated from Newcastle, challenged a smuggling cutter off Staithes. The vessel was sighted at anchor 'just a mile off the shore and was landing goods to many cobles'. The smuggling vessel quickly got under weigh and set sail towards the north. The *Lively* set off in hot pursuit but was soon outdistanced. The Commander, Thomas Brown, thought that the smuggling vessel was the *Good Endeavour*. The Excise Board had circulated information about this cutter; it was their belief that it had made several runs on the Lincolnshire coast and was captained by Fergus Murray, the ex-mate of a Scottish Excise vessel who had been dismissed from the Service for drunkenness and dishonesty! After about an hour or so the *Lively* gave up the chase and returned to Staithes. The ship's gig was launched with the intention of seizing the goods that had already been landed but obviously the villagers had other ideas.

The mate of the *Lively*, John Walford, has left a vivid report of the abortive landing:

'. . . as we neered the shore, we could see a goodly gathering of the country people they seemed most fierce and armed with sticks, bat and stones. We were very close when stones were thrown, so I ordered shots to be fired over the heads but this action occasioned a volley of pistols from them injuring two mariners. We were prevented from coming ashore by upwards of 50 people, who surrounded our boat and attempted to overturn it. The opposition was so strong and vicious that I deemed it hazardous to the safety of the mariners to proceed further . . . It is my belief that this place is very active in the trade.'

Walford and his boat crew managed to extricate themselves and return safely to the *Lively*. Walford was not an officer noted for his lack of determination or courage, as he later commanded the Excise cutter *Fly* from Harwich with quite commendable success and bravery, but he and his boat crew had now experienced the tenacity and ruthlessness of the Yorkshire smugglers, especially those at Staithes.

It would almost seem that the Whitby collector had given up on both Staithes and Runswick Bay, though in this respect he would have been little different to his colleagues at other ports along the east and south coasts. There were so few seizures of any note or consequence along the whole coast from Coatham to Runswick Bay from the 1780s until well into the next century that one is tempted to suggest that the whole of this coast was completely given over to the smugglers. The Government almost acknowledged this unpalatable fact by claiming, in 1783, that 'the illegal trade pervaded every city, town and village in the country, and brought distress and ruin to the honest trader'. Indeed figures were quoted that, even at this distance of time, seem almost incredible. It was estimated that 3,870,000 gallons of spirits, five to six million pounds of tea and one and a quarter million pounds of tobacco were smuggled into the country annually. Furthermore it was thought that over 50,000 persons were solely employed in smuggling with maybe a quarter of a million more engaged in the trade to a lesser degree. In 1781 Lord Pembroke asked, 'Will Washington take America; or the smugglers England first?, the bet would be a fair, even one'. And the Customs Board reiterated this view when they succinctly commented 'the smugglers carry on a system of business which set all the laws at defiance'!

However, with smuggling at an unprecedented height one of the Newcastle Customs cutters brought off one of the biggest coups. In October 1802 Captain Whitehead with his *Eagle* cutter captured, off Hunt Cliff Foot near Saltburn, a large smuggling lugger named *Resolution* after a chase which lasted nearly six hours. The lugger had been first sighted hovering off the

Holderness coast and the pursuit took the two vessels right up the Yorkshire coast. With some superb seamanship Whitehead drove his opponent close to the coast, until near Saltburn it became embayed. There was a sharp and rapid exchange of cannon shot and though little damage was done to either vessel, the smuggling lugger lowered its sails and surrendered. Whitehead returned to Newcastle in triumph, the *Resolution* was over 200 tons and had on board eleven bales of tobacco (910 pounds) and no less than 3,330 gallons of geneva. It was an American vessel, its home port was New York but on this occasion it had come from Hull via Holland. This is the only instance, to my knowledge, of an American vessel being seized for smuggling. It also shows that Hull had developed a flourishing trade with the Americas and the Indies by the beginning of the 19th century.

Marske continued to feature in the smuggling scene. Simon Collier, the riding officer there, found 'six tubs of geneva, 40 pounds of tobacco and a quantity of tea in the yard of Tobias Smith'. Collier reported that Smith stoutly maintained that he had been forced at pistol point to let his outbuilding be used by the smugglers. It would also appear that what Collier had found was just a small part of 'the landing made the previous night near here by a known smuggling gang . . .' – perhaps a veiled reference to Andrew? Maybe as a result of this information the Stockton collector, John Carr (James Carr's grandson), ordered Captain Holley on board the *Trial* to patrol the coast regularly from Hunt Cliff to Teesmouth where much smuggling business was still done. 'You are to correspond with the officers on land as they have the knowledge of the places and persons involved in this damaging trade . . .' At long last somebody in authority acknowledged that the riding officers had the best local knowledge, perhaps Carr had listened intently to his grandfather's stories! Not much is known about the *Trial* except that it was 'a decked vessel of just under 60 tons' but it was the first Customs vessel to operate from the Tees since the days of the ill-fated *Ferret.*

In November 1807 Collier searched 'Taylor's farm in Marske on information' – this is the only reference to information being received by the Customs in the area, perhaps at long last the tide was beginning to turn in their favour. Collier's initial search proved fruitless and presumably without the benefit of information he would have left it there. However, he had his suspicions about a newly erected cowshed and on closer examination he discovered a trapdoor concealed under a pile of straw. This door gave access to a specially constructed double wall affording a space of about six by four feet, which contained 23 bags of tobacco and four half-ankers of brandy. There was no doubt that the game was still being played but now the smugglers were using greater subterfuge to achieve their ends.

As far as Saltburn is concerned its name seems to disappear from the Customs records, certainly with regard to seizures. No doubt this is further evidence of the success of John Andrew, though it has been suggested that he did have the odd close call with the preventive men. For all the successful smugglers, and indeed they were relatively few, there were literally hundreds who were not so lucky and were caught and convicted, doomed to spend years in a debtor's prison, or worse, long service in the Royal Navy.

There was an old smuggling adage that 'Smuggling money never did good to anyone' and I suppose that Robert Calvert of Skelton might well subscribe to that view. He was a casual farm labourer who was convicted of petty smuggling in 1812. He petitioned the Customs Board for leniency and his appeal was supported by 'twenty people of Skelton including the curate and two churchwardens':

'[Skelton] is a poor labouring man with a wife and Family, who sorely depend upon your Petitioner for support and whom he has hitherto brought up in an honest and industrious way . . . [he] is not able to pay the Penalties incurred and that if the prosecution is carried out will end his days in a Gaol . . . [pray] accept the offer of Twenty pounds provided by the Charitable and human assistance of his Friends and Neighbours . . .'

Considering that the average annual wage at the time was not much in excess of £45, Calvert's penalty of £50 does seem rather harsh. Such petitions to the Customs Board were fairly frequent and they came mostly from the very small-time smuggler, the farm labourer-cum-lander, who only became involved to earn a little extra money and were very minor cogs in the smuggling trade. Nevertheless many spent several years in gaol with little or no hope of finding the money to pay off their debt, perhaps more importantly having no influential patron to plead their case.

With the advent of the preventive boats at Coatham and Staithes the smuggling trade began to be controlled for the first time for nearly a century. However, the sitter (coxswain) of the boat at Coatham complained bitterly that 'no houses in this area will provide lodgings . . .' This was not an unusual situation; b'ecause of the almost universal hostility of the local people it was virtually impossible to find suitable accommodation for the preventive boatmen. Furthermore the Customs Board also experienced great difficulty in obtaining land to build their watch-houses, local landowners were loath to sell! The Customs Board were therefore forced to seek compulsory purchase orders and the watch-houses they finally erected along the coasts contained living quarters as well as a place to store the boat. These buildings were the precursors of the Coastguard cottages built later in the century, some of which still stand today. The preventive boatmen at Coatham came from Yarmouth and those at Staithes from Dover. This was because of the Customs' age-old theory that bringing 'outsiders' into an area prevented collusion with the smugglers.

It is interesting to note that the Coatham preventive station was one of the first to be issued with Captain Manby's mortar rocket. This was basically a strong line attached to a shell which could be fired fairly accurately up to some 275 yards and was used for vessels in distress, thus introducing a life-saving element into their duties, which later became such a feature of the work of the Coastguard. The choice of Coatham for this new apparatus shows how dangerous this stretch of coast was to shipping.

But it was the establishment of Coastguard stations at Coatham, Saltburn, Hunt Cliff, Skinningrove and Staithes that saw the demise of smuggling and made the trade almost a memory of the past. As one traveller to the area observed in 1838, 'Smuggling now hardly pays on this coast but at Skinningrove the village gossips still talk about the golden age of smuggling and a certain parish clerk, who used to make the church steeple a hiding place for his contraband goods'. But perhaps the last words on smuggling in the area are best left with Alexander Dixon the Whitby collector, who maintained '. . . besides petty smuggling it has now been completely checked because of the exertions of the Coastguard'. The long and bitter battle had been won!

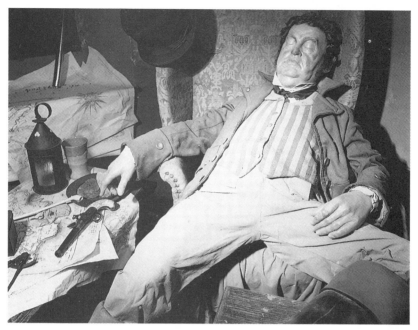

John Andrew 'resting', as depicted at the Saltburn Smugglers Heritage Centre
(Langbaurgh on Tees Borough Council)

Places to visit

The best way to visit this coast is from the A19, then the A1085
to Redcar. At about 2 miles from Redcar on the left-hand side of
the road you can see Coatham Marsh Bird Sanctuary and Nature
Reserve, which gives some idea of the area in smuggling days.

Before arriving at Redcar take the A1042 to the delightful and
historic village of Kirkleatham, the scene of many a smuggling
affray. This village has some fine buildings and a chapel. The **Old
Hall Museum**, an attractive Queen Anne building, has displays of
the maritime life of the area. Open 10 am to 5 pm from
Thursdays to Mondays, admission is free. Close by is the ancient
parish church of St Cuthbert with its rather unusual mausoleum.

Retrace your steps to Redcar itself, which is a bustling and
attractive resort. Well worth a visit is the **RNLI's Zetland Museum**
situated in the old Lifeboat House along the Esplanade. Open
11 am to 4 pm from May to September, admission is free and a car
park is provided.

From Redcar take the coast road to pass through Marske-by-the-Sea, another well-known smuggling village, before picking up the A174 to Saltburn-by-the-Sea. This rather charming Victorian resort is set high above the sea and shore and gives wonderful views of this famous smuggling coast. A trip down the oldest cliff tramway in Britain (there is a small token charge) brings you down to the promenade and a walk along the only pleasure pier in Yorkshire affords excellent views of the coast to the north and the south.

Take the A174 to Whitby and after a mile or so you will arrive at the Old Ship Inn and the **Saltburn Smugglers Heritage Centre.** This centre is a positive must, with an excellent exhibition well deserving its award by the British Tourist Authority in 1992. It is open seven days a week from Easter to the end of September, and at weekends only from 1st October, 10 am to 6 pm. There is an entrance fee. There is ample car parking close by. Also do not miss the small Victorian mortuary set alongside the main road near to the Centre.

After leaving Saltburn the A174 climbs steeply up to Hunt Cliff, where at Skinningrove the **Tom Leonard Mining Museum** at Deepdale has a most authentic and exciting mining display. Open from April to September daily from 1 pm to 5 pm. There is an entrance fee.

Signposted off the A174 is the road to Staithes. The car park is at the top of the town entailing a walk down to the lower village and harbour. Staithes is one of the most picturesque smuggling villages along the coast.

Returning to the A174 you soon pass through Hinderwell, where several Excise seizures were made. Then take the road marked to Runswick to visit another smuggling village and its lovely bay. Rejoin the A174 just before Ellerby and continue for about 2 miles before taking a country road to Goldsborough. Just beyond the village are the remains of the Roman signal station. You can then continue along the same road to Kettleness, 500 feet above the sea, where there is a Coastguard station overlooking Runswick Bay, and further along the cliff a Coastguard look-out affording spectacular views to the south.

4

From Sandsend to Ravenscar: 'A fine and comly coast'

From the Coastguard station perched high on Kettle Ness the view to the south extends as far as the promontory of Saltwick Nab which, jutting out into the North Sea, has been the cause of many a tragic shipwreck and is now under the care of the National Trust. This splendid panorama encompasses a rich variety of coastal scenery from the weathered cliffs above Sandsend, along the fine sweep of sands to Whitby where the ancient ruins high above the town dominate the scene and add a dramatic quality to the distant skyline.

Just about nine miles in length, this stretch of coast contains much of the history of the area – the Roman signal station, the old alum workings, the ancient port of Whitby and the Abbey. The old railway line, the disused quarries, the Coastguard lookouts, the twin lights of Whitby harbour and the lifeboat station are all vivid and intrinsic reminders of the rich maritime heritage of this particular part of the Yorkshire coast.

Then around the corner from Whitby lies the majestic sweep of Robin Hood's Bay with its eponymous town tumbling headlong down to the shore, hardly changed since its 'golden' days of smuggling. And in the far distance is Old Peak with its remnants of the alum trade. The more modern hilltop village of Ravenscar commands the peak and can probably claim to have one of the most spectacular coastal views in all Yorkshire. Without doubt an outstanding and beautiful stretch of coast, which one visitor described rather modestly as 'a fine and comly [sic] coast'. Besides its natural attributes it is also generously endowed with smuggling memories and legends.

19th century engraving of Whitby.

However, for centuries it has been Whitby, both as a town and a port, that has dominated the coast. One writer has suggested: 'The old town, though regarded with much admiration by the neighbouring villagers, and very progressive to the extent of its possibilities, was really only the petty metropolis of a primitive community shut in by the sea on one side and by wild moorlands on the other, satisfied with its local importance and caring little for anything beyond its limits'. True, its countrywide fame lasted probably no more than a century from 1750 to 1850, when whaling, ship-building and the jet and alum trade brought fortune and wealth to the town and port. It is no small coincidence that this period equates almost exactly with the heyday of smuggling, when Whitby and the neighbouring coast figured large in the free-trade. By the end of the 19th century Whitby had returned to a fairly quiet existence that relied on fishing, some summer visitors and past glories. There is a nice recollection of George du Maurier advising a prospective visitor in 1890 '. . . to see the forty or fifty cobles embark to the herring fishery, with all the town – men, women and children pushing the boats off . . .'.

The Customs presence in the port can be positively traced back to 1203 but in the late 17th century Allan Wharton, the collector, controlled his empire, which extended from Teesmouth to Old

88

This beautiful and unique stained glass portrait of Charles II was originally in the Whitby Custom House and is now proudly displayed in the Board Room of H.M. Customs and Excise in London.

Peak (Ravenscar), from the Custom House in St Ann's Staith on the edge of the old harbour in the north side of the town. It is not known for certain whether it was this building that displayed the very fine and unique stained glass portrait of Charles II, which is now a central feature of the Board Room of HM Customs and Excise in London. This portrait reminded visitors to the Whitby Custom House that the Customs was not only a Royal revenue but 89 that it was Charles II who founded the modern Customs service in 1671. It was at this Custom House that a circular letter from the Customs Board in London arrived on Wharton's desk in June 1673:

'It has come to the notice of Hons. Commissioners that many outrages are daily committed on the coasts of England, combed wool and woolfells are being regularly transported to foreign parts without the payment of the Revenues and proper cocquet [Customs seal] being applied. You are directed to search and seize all such wools, apprehend the owners thereof, if they are not able to give proper account of the same . . . It is also their Hons. Commissioners belief that foreign vessels are bigg in this trade and utmost care should be taken in clearing such vessels in your port and the officers under your management should be made aware of this immoral trade . . .'

This would be the first of many, many letters from London about the state and extent of smuggling. Of course this one referred to the age-old practice of wool smuggling out of the country, but there is no firm evidence that owling was a particular problem in Whitby though it would seem strange that a coast that took so readily to import smuggling during the 18th century would not also have been involved in the earlier trade, especially considering the extent of sheep farming on the moorlands that backed the coast.

It was not until the early 1720s that there is evidence of seizures of smuggled goods in Whitby and the nearby coast and this early evidence of smuggling just confirmed the pattern of the latter extensive free-trade activities. Sandsend, with its small harbour, was the centre of a thriving and active alum trade and the village was almost solely dependent on the industry. In January 1723 William Selby, the Customs surveyor at Whitby, found four ankers of brandy and two bags of tea packed on a horse, which was being led along the shore by a man called Patton. Both goods and horse were duly seized and auctioned for the grand sum of £73.10s. And just three months later Selby and a tidesman searched 'the house of Matthew Tindall at Sandsend' and they uncovered brandy, tea and salt hidden 'in a secret cupboard neath the stairs'. Though barely two miles from the Whitby Custom House Sandsend would prove to be a constant and nagging problem for the Customs, mainly due to the number of small colliers and alum vessels that used the little harbour. In 1750 no less than four alum vessels had been seized for smuggling but in all cases the vessels were released after the fines had been paid. The collector had this to say about the place in 1756: '. . . the prevalence of vessels coming to discharge and load there and the numbers of workers in the trade [alum] make it difficult to manage . . . the quantities that are landed begar description . . . my officers are tested to put a halt to this ruinous trade . . .'

But for all that, it was Robin Hood's Bay that was to prove the constant bane of every Whitby collector for at least the next 100 years. A small and rather insignificant incident in May 1722 seemed to set the format for all future relations between the Revenue and the Bay's men – in short truculence, insolence and violence. Richard Wilson, who had the unenviable post of riding officer for that part of the coast, seized two half-ankers of brandy from a Christopher Conniers. The collector's report succinctly sums up the confrontation:

'One anker wherof ye said Conniers took by violence from him [Wilson] in ye presence of his master, Jno Postgate, whom Wilson desired in his Majestie's Name to stay by him and order his servant Conniers away. Another anker ye said 'Conniers staved and split all ye Brandy after seizure and the remaining one the said Wilson with some difficulty did secure and was brought to his Majestie's warehouse . . .'

Twelve months later the collector informed London that he could not serve the 'attachment' for assault as Conniers had fled the area some time ago and 'even his master will not offer any information'. It took another twelve months before Conniers came back home. He was arrested by an under-sheriff and carted off to York Castle to await his trial. In this instance the long arm of the law was very patient. In later years when violence against Revenue officers became more commonplace persons like Conniers remained free with impunity.

Wilson did not seem too concerned about the incident because there are numerous references to his seizures in the area, though it must be admitted that they were very minor items and mostly found 'in the fields' rather than directly from persons. However, in May 1724, he did tackle two men, who were 'allom miners at the peak'; they tried to frighten Wilson – 'Thrattened me with a batte and pick but ran away when they see I was not to be moved'! 91

Two days later it is reported that he brought in another two half-ankers of brandy from 'under the cliffs at the Peak'. When one considers that the cliffs there are some 600 feet high, the journey down and back up must have been quite a formidable task. In the same month two Excise officers found three half-ankers of geneva and 100 pounds of tea in 'an ale-house in the Baytown . . . thought to have been run this sennight [week]'. There seems no doubt that these small and minor seizures were merely the tip of the iceberg, at least judged by the subsequent smuggling reputation of the town. However, there seemed to be enough smuggling going on in Whitby itself to give Hamlet Woods, the collector, plenty of sleepless nights.

One could be forgiven for assuming that just about everybody in the town was dabbling in the free-trade. During 1722, a half-anker of brandy was taken from a woman 'alongside the quayside [who] was unknown to the officer'. Then in June four stones of 'Pruenes' were taken from a master of a Whitby coble, who admitted that he had obtained them from a Dutch vessel at anchor in the bay. Prunes do seem a strange commodity to smuggle but they were liable to a high Customs duty – 12s per hundredweight, so the duty on these smuggled goods was only 6s – a minor sum but still almost one week's wage for most people. In September, Selby 'chased a coble up the river [Esk], she having taken goods from a vessel at sea, and when he came up with her he found the goods had been dropt. Edwin Hudson and 2 others being then in her'. Along the riverside Selby managed to recover eight half-ankers and one 'stoupe' (bottle or flagon) of brandy as well as some geneva. Then at the close of the year Abram Watkins, a tidesman, found five half-ankers of brandy in a coble 'at the end of the little pier' – perhaps a reference to the east pier, which was rebuilt in stone around about 1702.

In the following year (1723) there was a considerable number of seizures in various houses in the town – no less than 'seven cwts of iron in the shop of Richard Lotherington', nine half-ankers of brandy 'at widow Mary Marshall' and 15 half-ankers at 'the house of Dorothy Cumming'. The Whitby ladies appeared to be deeply involved in the free-trade. In September Adeline Huntrods had to swear on oath that she had 'bought the articles [which had been seized] in lawful trade, the Bed Tick at Whitby Fair, and the Flax at Guisborough, where it was manufactured and does verily

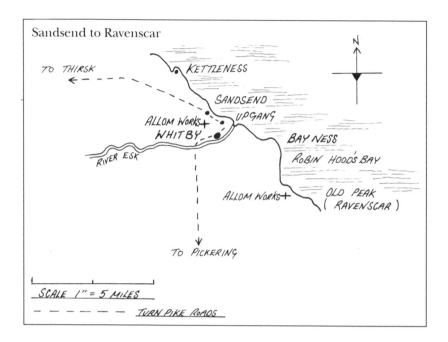

Sandsend to Ravenscar

TO THIRSK

KETTLENESS

SANDSEND

UPGANG

ALLOM WORKS

WHITBY

RIVER ESK

BAY NESS

ROBIN HOOD'S BAY

ALLOM WORKS

OLD PEAK
(RAVENSCAR)

TO PICKERING

SCALE 1" = 5 MILES

TURN PIKE ROADS

believe that the duties have been paid'! However, she was obviously a marked women because just two months later a half-anker of brandy was found in her house.

So concerned was the collector about the state of smuggling within the town that he petitioned the Customs Board to provide 'a nimble coble to patrol the river and nearby coast'. Since 1718, the surveyor had provided one at his own expense but 'ye same happening to be lost in a recent storm [January 1722]'. The cost of a 21 foot coble, which required four boatmen, came to 16 guineas. The vessel was finally authorised by London but only after Woods had sent two half-ankers of ale to the Head Office official, who was to make the final decision – obviously the ale helped to concentrate the mind! The coble was finally built locally, as was the normal procedure, but was slightly larger than first envisaged, 24 feet and requiring an extra boatman. Strangely, though all similar Customs boats were built in the respective ports, the specially made ash oars came from London; there was even a post of 'oar maker to the Board'!

The boat, at least when new, must have had a smart appearance, 93 painted black with a red trim and the King's Arms emblazoned on the backboard. From 1721 all Customs were required to fly the Revenue jack – a red flag with the Union Jack in one corner and in the main field a castellated portcullis – whilst on patrol. It would certainly have been a most distinctive vessel, and deliberately so to ensure that smugglers could not plead mistaken identity when challenged. This had its disadvantages, at some ports the Customs vessels suffered malicious damage at the hands of smugglers!

Having at long last obtained his new coble, the collector had to admit ruefully that 'can't yet find one man or boy yet is willing to go to sea with your vessel, either in this town or nearby'. Customs boatmen received an annual salary of £15 with a daily allowance when employed, certainly not overpaid for the dangers they faced or for the unpopularity of their calling, though they could expect to increase their income by rewards for seizures. They were required to be 'lusty and hardy men . . . well bred to the sea [with] an honest Christian faith'. There is no doubt that their work was the most arduous in the service, which is reflected in the number of them who were prematurely retired because in contemporary jargon they were worn out or of no further use. Of course, in a port like Whitby there were ample attractive alternatives in the fishing and coal trades to encourage young men who wished to go to sea (as James Cook did) without the strong monetary incentive of smuggling.

An example of the violence that they were likely to face is shown by what happened to Abram Watkins in March 1723 when he was 'on watch at a place called Cliff field [better known now as Upgang] . . . between 11 and 12 o'clock at night when I did meet Richard Stonehouse and Stephen Greg, Coblemen, with each of them half-anker of brandy. Whereupon I charged them to deliver in ye King's name, so they threw them to the ground; whereupon perceiving I had no assistance, the said Richard Stonehouse struck me heavily to the face and then held me by force until Stephen Gregg ran away with one of ye half-ankers and the other I brought to ye Custom House with much difficulty'. For hanging about on a cold and inhospitable shore and suffering some indignity and slight injury, Watkins received the princely sum of 1s as a seizure reward for the brandy. It is hardly surprising that there was no queue of aspiring applicants outside the Custom House! However, the collector did finally manage to crew his coble, though some of the boatmen were not that young or 'lusty'.

It was in the port itself that the biggest seizures were made. In June 1724 Selby was just going on board the Whitby vessel *George and Juno*, which had recently arrived from the Netherlands, when he met the master, George Cockerill, and his wife coming ashore. 'I seized 10 yards Muslin and 8 handkerchiefs. I also saw a coble putting off from her deep laden with goods but was not able to come up with her. The master came back on board at once saying that he was bound for Norway and would not suffer any goods to be taken from her but after some resistance, I brought away and secured 29 pounds of tea and a half-anker of brandy. Also 7 half-ankers White Wine, 1 half-anker Sack and one piece of Holland linen'. Not a bad haul but there was no question of the vessel being seized as well as the goods. In 1718 it was enacted that brandy brought in on any vessel under 15 tons would be seized and the vessel forfeit to the Crown – hence the reason so many Yorkshire cobles were forfeited.

A fine imbroglio occurred at the port in August of the same year, starting very innocently as the *Sarah and Grisell* entered the harbour and berthed at St Anne's Staith – very close to the Custom House. The master, Thomas Robertson, reported that he had come from Perth and had only come into port for fresh provisions and because of stress of weather – there was a storm brewing in the North Sea. However, a report was received from Richard Wilson saying that the vessel had been seen hovering in Robin Hood's Bay and 'selling spirits to the fishing cobles from the sea'. The collector therefore decided to organise a rummage of the vessel and as a result his officers found the hold filled with salt in which was buried a considerable number of brandy ankers. Apparently some had already been landed as 'the vessel was lightened above half a foot forward'.

On being questioned the master changed his story, he now claimed that he had sailed from St Martin in France en route to Bergen with a cargo of salt and brandy. Then on the following evening when the tide and the weather were favourable, Robertson decided to cut his losses and slip out of the harbour. Now there would have been at least one tidesman on board by day and night whilst any import cargo was still on board. The Customs men realised that the vessel was being made ready for sea, yelled out for assistance and several of their colleagues managed to get on board but 'despite all ye fair means the officers could use, the Master ordered his men to cast off the mooring'. Then ensued a battle between the Customs and the crew as they tried to prevent them setting the sails and they even attempted to unship the rudder. The vessel was being towed by a local coble commanded by Christopher Hill 'a well-known smuggler', who shouted that he would murder every Customs officer. Selby, who was in the thick of the fray, was 'assaulted, opposed, resisted, molested, obstructed, hindered and abused' by the master and the mate. Selby's clothes were torn as 'he endeavoured to get the management of the helm in order to put the vessel on shore and at other times when he tried to obstruct their design'.

Despite all the valiant efforts of the Customs men the vessel edged slowly down the harbour, all the while they received 'severe abuse from the great number of people on the shore and from the cobles running alongside'. They were so heavily pelted with stones that they had to shelter behind the masts. The lusty Abram Watkins was well to the fore, he managed to cut some of the towing ropes despite being violently assaulted by the master. However, the Customs' delaying tactics proved successful, the tide had turned and the vessel ran aground 'in Collier Hope'.

After all the fuss had died down Selby maintained that Hill had threatened to fight him without the least provocation and that a large stone thrown from Hill's coble would have 'brained him' had he not deflected it with his arm. Another search of the vessel revealed 13 more casks of brandy and a parcel of playing cards. Prosecutions were prepared against the master, mate and Hill, but unfortunately the outcome is not known. It is most unlikely that the vessel was seized because then only vessels of 50 tons or under were liable to seizure if they were found 'hovering' within two leagues of the coast (about six miles). This was the first of many such Hovering Acts passed during the century and did, in fact, become the backbone of smuggling legislation.

In 1729 the collector had a very important visitor from Head Office in London; he was Walter Kettleby, the Inspector of east coast ports. Such port inspections were normal practice and often lasted several days during which every aspect of the business of the port was examined in great detail and a full report was sent back to the Customs Board. Kettleby really found little untoward though he did point out that the collector did not have a 'King's chest' to secure the official monies, instead he took them home for safe keeping! The design of these chests, many of which have survived, was based on the strong-boxes used by the Hanseatic League. Their special feature was the very complicated lock mechanism, located under the lid, which had a spring of great power operating up to eleven bolts. Being wrought-iron they were extremely heavy and cumbersome but some collectors put stones in them to make them even less portable.

The main interest of Kettleby's report is that it gives a valuable insight into the port, its officers and smuggling in the area:

'. . . this is a fine and comly [sic] coast . . . a prosperous port, well-tended quays with coal, fish and the Northern trade figures large in the Revenue . . . at the coasts the Allom business is very considerable and causes much trouble to the Collector, who appears a brisk & upright officer . . . the Surveyor, Wm. Selby is of good experience and makes much influence on the Smuggling trade, wch to all accounts in the port is increasing on the coasts . . . to the south is a most hazardous district [Robin Hood's Bay] where running of goods is commonplace, its people show a strong disregard for his Majesty's Revenue . . . and to the north, where there is a goodly trade in coal and stone and some frauds are committed . . . The Colltr, has remarked on the number of foreign ships that use the coasts to unshipp cargoes . . . an armed cruiser would prevent such insults to the fair trade . . .'

Kettleby left the collector with detailed instructions on the proper rummaging of vessels, which were to be copied to every member of staff.

These instructions were really quite amazing as they detailed the various contrivances used on vessels to conceal smuggled goods – false bulkheads, compartments hollowed out of cabins, hollow masts and other hiding places. They also gave clear directions on the proper use of spits to search cargo and ballast for hidden goods. Most writers on smuggling have attributed such devices to the so-called scientific period of smuggling dating from 1820 onwards, and yet almost 100 years earlier there is evidence that even then such methods were well known and presumably well used. Copies of these instructions were issued by most Customs inspectors on their visits to other ports, so there was no excuse if such smuggling contrivances went undetected.

It would be good to say that the seizure record of the port   97

'Old Smuggler', Baxtergate, Whitby – previously the 'Ship Launch Inn'.

improved as a result of the inspection but alas that was not so, in fact it so deteriorated that six years later the collector was asked to explain why the number of prosecutions had fallen. One obvious answer to an outsider is that William Selby had retired and his replacement was certainly not as active or enthusiastic. Hamlet Woods, however, preferred to lay the blame with the local Justices, who according to him 'had absolutely refused to give any penalties and gave this their reason "that when persons are worth nothing, by confining them the Publick loses the benefit of their labour and have their families to keep during the confinements [in prison]"'. The two Justices in question were Hugh Cholmley, Lord of the Manor, and Robert Linskill, an important merchant in the town. Such a view was unique and not put forward as an explanation anywhere else in the country. Most collectors found that they could not obtain satisfactory prosecutions because local Justices seemed to sympathise with the smugglers and usually found in their favour.

On the other hand the Excise officers were not quite so dilatory or perhaps they were just a bit more lucky. In January 1756 an Excise officer stopped three men on the road out of Sandsend, who were moving some landed goods. The men decided to make a stand and started to attack with loaded whips and an iron bar. Despite being badly bruised and shaken the Excise man managed to fire both his pistols which, although the shots missed his assailants, frightened them sufficiently to take to their heels and disappear into the woods. A local innkeeper was co-opted into storing the geneva, tea and chocolate overnight. No less than four Excise men arrived the following morning to carry the goods to the Excise warehouse in Whitby. This was said to be near Market Place in the old part of the town and near to the Custom House, which had now moved to a new building in Sandgate.

Later in the same year two Excise officers found a quantity of tea and coffee in an inn in the port, which was said to have been hidden under sacks in an outhouse. The name of the inn was not disclosed; it could have been the Ship Launch Inn in Baxtergate, which had a reputation as a haunt of smugglers, but undoubtedly there were other inns in the town which could have made similar claims. The old inn still stands, though nowadays it is a café that goes under the name of the Old Smuggler but it still retains a fine if somewhat worn figurehead on the outside wall. This is reputed to have once belonged to a smuggling vessel that was broken up by the Customs. The claim that its presence was there as a warning to all smugglers seems a rather tall story!

Some idea just how far the smuggled goods managed to penetrate into the county is shown by two other Excise seizures. One was made from a John Wilson, a pedlar or chapman, near Aislaby which is close to Pickering and over 20 miles from Whitby. Throughout the country the ubiquitous packmen or chapmen were notorious for dealing in smuggled goods. Wilson had a quantity of 'Holland lace and linen' as well as some French cambric. He admitted that he had bought the goods from a Whitby woman but of course did not know her name!

A larger seizure was made in May 1769 when a farm wagon was stopped on a road out of Thirsk, nearly 35 miles from the coast. There were six half-ankers of geneva, two of brandy and 30 pounds of tea hidden under straw. The two farm labourers maintained that they did not know where the goods had been landed but had picked them up at Helmsley from a John Hathersage, who they thought came from Baytown. The goods and the wagon were seized and somebody paid the £30 penalty each was fined.

The Whitby seamen and probably most of the merchants were deeply involved in the free-trade and the smuggled goods appeared to be mainly brought in by the legally trading vessels – at least according to the Customs records, and colliers seemed to be particularly active in the trade. In March 1770 a Shields collier *Trinity* arrived with a cargo of coal from the Tyne but it had 30 half-ankers of geneva, six bales of tobacco and 150 pounds of tea all of which were hidden underneath the coal. The master was adamant that he knew nothing of the goods and blamed his crew, or rather three of them who were Whitby bred – the implication being that they had family connections in the port. However, it was thought that the smuggled goods had originated from one of 'the number of smuggling vessels that ply the coast, especially to the north'. It is not clear how the master explained away this fact.

Almost a year later a Whitby collier *Hannah and Jane* arrived with hemp and flax from Denmark. Everything appeared quite normal until about a week after its arrival when the mate, Moses Hardiman was stopped alongside the quayside. He was carrying four flagons of wine, six canisters of tea and a small quantity of

19th century engraving of Robin Hood's Bay.

tobacco. It was then decided to rummage the vessel; whether this was done on arrival is not stated, but the subsequent search revealed six casks of wine, tobacco and snuff and ten canisters of tea. The goods were said to have been concealed in the sails' locker and in the cabins underneath the cots. The collector admitted that 'the tidesman was slack in his attention to his duties'; this was probably a euphemism for him being drunk or asleep or even both! Though in fairness the crew were allowed to take their beds on board and also their wives if they so wished – the latter practice was only discontinued in the 1820s! Such smuggling was almost impossible to prevent especially in a port like Whitby where the quays were right in the centre of the town.

But despite all the problems that were present in the port, there was no doubt whatsoever that John Burgh, Woods' successor, considered his greatest headache was Robin Hood's Bay. In February 1772 Horatio Roberts, a Whitby port officer, searched William Cobb's house and found 'below stairs upon a bed where Cobb and his wife usually lie 2 ankers of geneva, 4 bags of tea and 14 bags in another place. In another room 6 canisters under the garret stairs. In an open closet 35 pounds of tea and in an

Robin Hood's Bay from the top of the town.

adjoining chamber 12 canisters of tea. Mrs Cobb told the officer that she was privy to the goods being lodged there'. Less than three weeks later the same officer seized 20 bags of tobacco, ten canisters of tea and six pitchers of geneva from the house of John Haversome – probably the same person who supplied the two farm labourers in 1769. All the goods were said to be hidden in various closets and cupboards throughout the dwelling.

There are several interesting points to these two seizures. First they seem to prove the long-held view that most of the houses and cottages in Robin Hood's Bay had secret cupboards and hiding places. Also it would seem very likely that the collector had received information about both Cobb and Haversome as the search of houses was not undertaken without strong evidence.

Furthermore it is known that the collector had paid money to informers out of his own pocket because he later asked Head Office how he could claim the money from his official accounts! Perhaps the most intriguing element is why a senior Whitby officer should be sent to undertake the searches. Despite his official title – a searcher – he was solely concerned with the supervision and examination of imported goods. One wonders why John Robinson,

102

the riding officer, did not figure in the search.

This matter becomes much clearer by the following March when the collector was informed that the Customs Board in London had received an anonymous letter about the 'phenomenal extent of smuggling in Robin Hood's Bay' which also included an accusation that 'the Customs there are concerned, encouraged and received gratification for permitting that pernicious trade'. Obviously Robinson was asked to explain but unfortunately his reply to the charges has not survived, if indeed one was ever written! Certainly by 1774 he was replaced by a Thomas May but I feel that John Burgh had his suspicions of Robinson all along, which may explain why Roberts was sent to conduct the rummages.

There is no doubt that the Bay was regularly used by a variety of smuggling vessels. In October 1773 there were no less than a schooner, a cutter and two shallops all landing goods in the Bay. When the two Customs cutters – *Mermaid* and *Eagle* – appeared upon the scene, the four vessels 'shot out of the bay' and proceeded to attack and run off the Customs vessels. Captain Whitehead of the *Mermaid* identified one of the shallops as the *Porcupine* commanded by the infamous 'Smoker' Browning. The schooner was not named but was thought to be commanded by Michael Connell or Conett – 'a well-known smuggler'. Four years later the *Swallow*, a Customs vessel from Hull with Captain Mitchell in command, was allowed to approach close to the *Porcupine*, which was busy supplying cobles. Browning waited until the *Swallow* was within musket range before he fired a fusillade and warned Mitchell off in no uncertain terms using very ripe language! The *Swallow* was the smallest Customs vessel operating along the Yorkshire coast; it was less than 100 tons with a crew of 14 men, just four two-pound cannons and a handful of swivels. It was certainly no match for vessels of the size of the *Porcupine*.

The state of smuggling and the utter disregard and contempt for the Revenue forces along the coast brought a strong condemnatory notice in the *Yorkshire Gazette* in April 1774:

'The practice of smuggling increases amazingly in these parts. It has become so general that seizures are almost daily made, and many people of supposed good circumstances are known to deal largely in the pernicious trade. If the contraband trade is suffered to go on it will inevitably drain the County of a great part of its money and endanger the lives and morals of its inhabitants.'

It might be a trifle cynical to suggest that this notice had some influence on the decision by the War Office to send troops to Whitby to provide support for the Revenue forces. As already mentioned, John Burgh had sent at least three petitions to London on the matter. Finally a detachment of the Royal British Dragoons arrived at the end of 1774. Mr J. Clarke, the constable at Robin Hood's Bay, was told that a non-commissioned officer and six dragoons and their horses 'will march to your place where you must take care to quarter them in the best manner you can for their accommodation and also give them what assistance that is within your power and duties'. Two dragoons were billeted at Sandsend, the rest going to Staithes and Runswick Bay with dire results (see Chapter Three). There is no evidence whatsoever to show that they had any material effect on the smuggling trade in the Bay, except possibly in the preventive sense; the most that can be said is that their presence in the town must have made the landing of goods that much more hazardous. It is not known how long they stayed but in August 1785 a squadron of the 6th Inskilling Regiment was directed into the area, presumably as the dragoons' replacement.

Another report in the *Yorkshire Gazette* featured a smuggling incident that was nothing short of a battle between the Excise and the Baymen. In October 1779, a group of Excise officers seized 260 casks of brandy and geneva, 15 bags of tea and a chest full of blunderbusses, pistols and cutlasses in Robin Hood's Bay. The town's smuggling fraternity were not prepared to allow this to happen and decided to fight back strongly, recovering all but ten casks and ten bags of tea. It was a brutal fight with no quarter given on either side. The townsmen were assisted by the crew of a smuggling vessel *Dover*, which had just arrived in the Bay; this band of smugglers were certainly not going to miss such a fight! It was reported that 'they had just broken into the Hartlepool Custom House'. The Hartlepool Custom House had indeed been broken into but that happened almost two years earlier – in November 1777 – when the crew of a smuggling vessel (not named) led by William Rowles succeeded in rescuing a cargo of tea and coffee that had previously been seized from them.

Custom Houses seemed a valid target, there are instances of break-ins in Colchester, King's Lynn, Yarmouth and the most famous – at Poole. Reportedly this smuggling crew paraded around Robin Hood's Bay greatly celebrating their victory over the Excise, but when they heard that a party of the Cumberland Militia, under the command of a Captain Barnes, was marching on the town from Whitby, they rapidly dispersed and disappeared in such a hurry that they left most of the firearms lying around the streets. Such reports as these, and they were frequent, fully justified Crabbe's view that the smugglers had gained 'a lawless passport through the land'. It is worth commenting here that in 1778 the notorious David 'Smoker' Browning finally met his match off St Albans Head in Dorset in a fight with the *Kite*, a Revenue cutter from Southampton. Browning was taken and after being found guilty was impressed into the Navy.

Robin Hood's Bay still continued to figure large in the Customs records. The problem this time was a certain 'Captain' David Pickney, who had a reputation as a notorious smuggler. In 1795 there was an outstanding prosecution against him for obstructing the officers of the Revenue in the execution of their duty. It was heard that he was back in town so two riding officers accompanied the constable to serve the warrant for his arrest, but this was returned unserved because '. . . of the irresolution of the Constable of Robin Hood's Bay . . . Pickney had fastened the door of his dwelling-house and barred the windows. He threatened the officers with a shot-gun should they attempt to take him . . .'. The constable was not prepared to take any further action as he considered his life was in grave danger. He also reasoned that as Pickney was 'on the point of going back to sea' it all seemed a pointless exercise, an opinion which was shared by the two riding officers! So Pickney escaped scot-free.

The Customs Board had long recognised that 'women are not immune from the smuggling trade'. As early as 1746 they issued a general letter to all ports which suggested that 'women passengers especially carry customable goods about their person'. They recommended that a woman in whom the collectors 'could confide in should act as a woman searcher'. There is no evidence that such a post existed at Whitby but most non-passenger and other small ports solved the problem by calling upon the services of the 105 wives of tide-waiters, most of whom had a fair knowledge of the workings of the Service gained from their attendance on vessels whilst accompanying their husbands. Certainly there did seem a desperate need for a woman searcher in Whitby during 1800 when there were several seizures made from townswomen. A certain Eliza Howard appeared to be running a rather nice profitable business in smuggled goods from her house. The Customs surveyor found tea, chocolate, geneva, lace and cambrics, admittedly not in great quantities but enough to suggest that she was a well-known supplier in the town. Another woman, Beth Howlett, was stopped alongside the quayside and 'in her basket were tea, coffee and tobacco', which was believed to have come from the *John and George*, a Newcastle collier that had just left the port on the evening tide. Mary O'Brian, who was described as a market woman was under grave suspicion by the Customs but it was not until late October that a small quantity of tea and geneva was found in her house; it was then maintained that she had 'been active in the trade for some time past and is believed to have sold such goods on market days . . .'.

Mrs Gaskell, the famous Victorian novelist, had most decided views on the subject:

'The clever way in which certain [Whitby] women managed to bring in prohibited goods; show how in fact when a woman did give her mind to smuggling, she was more full of resources and tricks and impudence and energy than any man.'

Considering that Mrs Gaskell spent time in Whitby during 1859 undertaking assiduous research for *Sylvia's Lovers,* her novel of Whitby (which she called Monkshaven) in its whaling days, I feel that she must have heard and been told endless smuggling stories and experiences and some, no doubt, at first hand and that she certainly can be considered a most credible witness. From my knowledge there is no comparable evidence of quite so much smuggling by women in other ports in the country, so Whitby women seemed to be most enterprising and indeed a breed apart.

In February 1803 Sir Charles Turner, a well-known member of the local gentry, caused quite a stir in Whitby and the neighbourhood when he publicly boasted that he could obtain claret at the very low price of 1s 6d a bottle; and moreover he further condemned himself when he offered to accommodate his

106

friends at the same rate. The outcry in the town was considerable and despite his elevated position in society some townspeople somewhat hypocritically suggested that 'such a delinquent should be brought to public shame for being involved in so infamous a transaction'. Sir Charles' statement must have been an acute embarrassment for the Whitby collector; indeed Sir Charles could have been prosecuted under an Act of 1779, which made those buying smuggled goods liable to a penalty of £10 for each separate offence and the supplier of the goods to a fine of £50. The Act also deliberately encouraged the practice of informing because it provided that if the seller gave evidence against the buyer within 20 days, and before any information had been laid against himself, then he would be absolved for his own offence. So the purchase of smuggled goods did present a certain risk. But there is no evidence to show that Sir Charles was ever prosecuted, nor were any of his counterparts around the country, of which there were many. Like much of English justice, the smuggling acts were rigorously applied only to the less fortunate members of society.

John Pitts, who had taken over as collector in 1806, replied to a letter that he had received from Lieutenant-General Pye in November 1807 enquiring about smuggling in his area:

'Sir, Yr. letter 10th inst. in answer, the town of Robinhood's Bay and Staithes are the general rendezvous for large vessels such as cutters and luggers employed in smuggling. They generally make for one of these places when they first come on the coast and where the principal agents reside who direct all the branches of this illicit traffick. On the arrival of the smuggling vessels on the coasts the agents send around secret notice thereof to the different people concerned in smuggling who assemble at the landing place where a large proportion of the smuggled goods is taken immediately into the interior of the country by the people by the numerous footpaths that the adjoining moors and hilly country affords. The remainder is secreted among the inhabitants of the towns and villages upon the coast and I am afraid that every facility is given to the smuggler by almost all the lower class of people and I am sorry to add by the large proportion of the higher ranks of society [Sir Charles Turner and his ilk] in this part of the country. I would recommend strong detachments of Military at Robinhood's Bay and Staithes frequently relieved to prevent too great an intercourse between the privates and the inhabitants as I am well aware that every species of temptation will be thrown out to them to induce them to neglect their duty.'

SMUGGLING IN YORKSHIRE

An interesting report which shows that smuggling had not greatly
changed over the years. However, what is really surprising is that
the military enquired about the state of smuggling considering
that hitherto they had only provided very grudging support to the
Customs. To understand this vastly different attitude it is necessary
to examine the position in which Great Britain found itself in late
1807. Prussia had been defeated by Napoleon and in November
1806 he issued his famous Berlin Decree, which began the
effective blockade of Britain. All commerce and correspondence,
whether carried in British or neutral ships was forbidden under
pain of death in all the lands controlled by France. The whole of
the continent of Europe from the Baltic to Turkey was closed to
British shipping except to the smuggling vessels. As Wordsworth
wrote: '. . . And we are left, or shall be left alone; the last that dare
struggle with the foe'. A high level decision was made that if the
country was to be blockaded then the 'treacherous' smugglers
should be prevented from trading as well. It was ordered that
'Every effort and design should be given to halt the traitorous
trade.' Throughout the country there was a perceptible fall-off of
seizures but this was not necessarily as a result of an increased
guard and vigilance along the coasts but by less smuggling taking
place – not all smugglers were prepared to trade with the enemy.
As it is known that Napoleon managed to supply his frozen army
in Poland with at least 50,000 West Riding overcoats and 200,000
Northampton boots, perhaps smuggling out of the country once
more became more profitable!

According to many local sources the most notorious smuggling
inn around Whitby was the Mulgrave Castle Inn, set high on the
cliff top about halfway between Sandsend and Whitby at a place
now known as Upgang. Certainly in those days it was in a prime
position but because of coastal erosion the inn and the cluster of
small cottages near it finally disappeared into the sea in 1887. But
in the early 1800s the landlady, Jane Bell, was reputed to be deeply
involved in the free-trade and it was said that many a landed
cargo had passed by its doors and I have no doubt that some must
have strayed inside the premises! It was in late autumn that a
smuggling lugger *Grey Dove* landed a considerable quantity of
geneva onto the beach at Upgang and this was quickly moved
away and hidden in two caves that were said to be situated in the
cliff face and concealed behind a long retaining stone wall.

108

The fine stretch of sands between Sandsend and Whitby, the scene of many a smuggling run.

The vessel returned the following night with another consignment of goods, which had been supplied by a large Dutch vessel hovering safely out to sea beyond the six mile limit. As so often happened one of the landers – a Whitby man – got himself slightly the worse for drink and openly boasted about his part in the affair. News was passed to the Customs, his house was searched and some geneva was found. He claimed that this had come from a fisherman who in turn had purchased it from a Dutch vessel. The preventive men were not totally convinced and a large-scale 109 search was made of houses in Whitby and the shore between Sandsend and Whitby. By sheer good fortune the Customs men found one of the caves, which contained a large quantity of casks. Wagons and horses were requisitioned to move the seized goods into Whitby, but the news of the large seizure travelled very quickly and by the time the train of wagons had arrived at Sandgate – the narrow street in the old part of the town where the Custom House was situated – a large and fairly angry crowd had gathered. There was much verbal abuse from the crowd and this quickly turned to a more physical nature as the Customs were jostled and in the struggle some of the casks were stolen, many were spiked and others were stove in. The geneva was soon flowing freely into the street and gutters, much to the delight of the raucous crowd; it was said that less than half the total of spirits were finally stored in the Custom House.

The following day another search was made of the houses of known trouble-makers and it was decided to mount another search of the stone wall. Although nothing of any consequence was found in the town because the goods had been too well distributed, the second cave was found. Unfortunately for the Customs this was empty but reportedly there was a message roughly chalked on the cave wall: 'Look here and Weep. 300 tubs taken from here last night'. A most frustrating two days for the Customs, who had been made to look very foolish indeed.

Despite this infuriating setback the initiative was being slowly and inexorably wrested away from the smugglers, but old habits die hard. The preventive boat at Robin Hood's Bay found sufficient evidence that the trade, although dying, was not quite dead. The boat station was sited at Wayfoot, a really prime position on the foreshore; its very presence there must have militated against widespread smuggling. The crew spent much of their time patrolling inshore along the Bay and they were rewarded for the efforts as they did pick up the odd cask of geneva and a few bales of tobacco, but in no great quantity. Perhaps the sitter of the boat summed up the situation rather succinctly when he said 'They hate the very sight of us but we have them worried we've stopped their game . . .'.

In April 1820 they did find 20 casks of geneva 'floating in the water secured by sinking stones', and another 25 casks hidden along the shore at Hawsker Bottom, which was said to be one of

110

the favourite landing spots along the Bay. The Whitby preventive boat was used mainly to the north of the port, their regular area of patrol extended to just beyond Sandsend. Then with the formation of the Coastguard in 1823 there were three officers and ten men based at Whitby with other men stationed elsewhere along the coast.

The trade was undergoing a subtle change. Slowly the country came to realise that smuggling was no longer the honest and romantic activity of yesterday but more a crime conducted against society in general. Perhaps the judgement in a famous smuggling case in Kent in 1826 had a considerable bearing on this changed outlook. The judge's actual words were:

> '. . . pleaded guilty to an offence of the most heinous nature, which struck terror into every well-disposed mind. It must be made known throughout the country that if an offence of this nature were again committed no mercy would be shown to the offenders . . . If persons in the highest stations of life were not to purchase smuggled goods there could be an end to smuggling, but many people laboured under the delusion that defrauding the revenue was no crime. It was a serious offence against the laws of God and smuggling led to the Commission of the greatest crime, that of murder.'

With such an outright condemnation of the illegal trade the days of large-scale smuggling were certainly numbered.

At sea the battle with the smuggling vessels was also being won. There were well over 30 strongly armed cutters operating around the coast. Many of these cutters had been newly built and the Customs Board had used some of the most famous boat builders of the time; Thomas Inman of Lymington, Ransom and Ridley of Hastings and Samuel White of Cowes had all gained fine reputations for speedy elegant yachts and they used their experience and expertise to produce some very fast Revenue cutters, which were more than equal opposition to the smuggling vessels. The officers and crews of these cutters were mainly ex-Naval men, few of the old Customs commanders survived the transfer to the Coastguard. And admittedly the Coastguard cutters were managed and operated in a much more professional manner. There were two cutters both based at Newcastle and Hull.

One of these was the *Mermaid* which operated from Newcastle, not the old *Mermaid* but a new cutter built by White at Cowes. 111

Though not large it was reputed to be very fast and for its size strongly armed with six carronades. These lightly constructed short-barrelled guns could fire a comparatively large shot a short distance. They were very effective at short range and at point blank range (about 400 yards) they were devastating enough to earn themselves the nickname 'the smasher'. The *Mermaid* was commanded by an ex-Naval lieutenant – Michael Harris – said to be a veteran of Trafalgar. In July 1823 it captured a smuggling lugger just off Whitby. The vessel had on board over 2,000 gallons of geneva, 2,100 pounds of tobacco and six and a half pounds of tea. The six man crew all claimed to be 'Belgians' though Belgium was not recognised as a separate kingdom until 1839, but whether Dutch or Belgian they were not liable to prosecution under the smuggling acts because they were foreign residents. Later it was discovered that two of them were in fact Englishmen and they were sentenced to five years in the Navy; they were the last smugglers along the Yorkshire coast to suffer this kind of punishment. Impressment of seamen had been slowly declining since 1815 because of the rundown of the Fleet, but nevertheless it was never formally abolished.

Not only was the scale of smuggling decreasing but its character was also changing. The days of the large English smuggling luggers appeared to be a thing of the past – at least on the Yorkshire coast. In the Customs records there are hardly any references to English vessels operating along the coast. Those arrogant and truculent smugglers of previous days – Browning, Fagg and the rest were being replaced by foreign smugglers, mainly Dutch and French, who with their vessels decided to test the strength and efficiency of the Coastguard at sea. But nevertheless they still seemed to need the co-operation of the locals because few seemed prepared to take the risk to land their own cargoes.

However, the exception proves the rule. In May 1824, one Dutch vessel tried to run some goods with rather disastrous results. The *Goede Hoope* was seized by Lieutenant King and his Coastguard boatmen whilst it was landing a cargo of spirits, tobacco and a small quantity of tea on the shore about one and a half miles north of Whitby – Upgang featuring once again! In this operation the Coastguard had been assisted by two Whitby pilots, a positive sign that the public attitude to smuggling was changing. The small quantity of tea proved to be the last recorded instance of this commodity being smuggled on the Yorkshire coast. The quite drastic reduction in import duty just showed what effect it could have on smuggling. Just two months later another Dutch vessel, the *Francois* from Ostend, was brought into Whitby after being taken near Runswick Bay with a consignment of spirits and tobacco. The foreign crews of both vessels ended up in York Castle because they could not pay the £100 fine imposed on each crew member. One unfortunate preventive officer was hurt in the engagement; he accidentally wounded himself in his thigh with one of his pistols and the shot had to be extracted by a Whitby surgeon.

The Whitby collector considered that 'the recent Act of Parliament which makes foreigners liable to the same penalties as Englishmen if caught smuggling has tended more to suppress the traffic than anything that has ever been done'. Although admittedly foreign smugglers had caused considerable problems along the Yorkshire coast in the past, I think he had rather overstated the case but perhaps he had allowed those two recent seizures to cloud his judgement. Indeed just a couple of weeks later he was bemoaning the fact that because the local magistrates 'were very reluctant to commit smugglers', he was experiencing considerable problems in securing convictions. His letter to London pleaded for 'a professional to conduct court proceedings'. The Customs Board replied somewhat tartly that the solution was in his own hands as he should ensure that 'any evidence brought by his officers was absolute and positive such as to demand a conviction'! However, they did concede that if he still encountered problems, he should furnish them with the names of the 'recalcitrant justices' when they would take such action as they thought fit, though they did not specify what they would do!

The Coastguard in the area appeared to be having a most positive effect on smuggling, obviously posing a very strong deterrent to the trade. In June 1834 *La Saint Marie*, a small French fishing vessel, was taken in Whitby Roads with brandy and tobacco on board and the eight man crew were all convicted, fined £100 each and as they were unable to find such a large sum they were taken to Northallerton Correction House under a guard of no less than eight Customs men – they were obviously taking no chances.

By 1850 the Inspector of the Coastguard at Whitby could report that although there was still some petty smuggling undertaken by French fishing vessels 'during the herring season' and that there

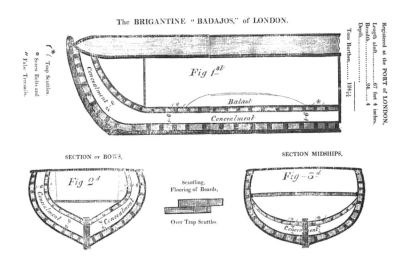

A typical concealment arrangement, similar to that used by the *John and Susannah*.

had been some landings of tobacco on 'the Staithes station', the coast under his command was really 'very quiet'. He concluded with the opinion that 'there is no disposition of the country people to renew smuggling, which must be occasioned by the zeal and vigilance of the officers under my command'. One can almost hear his audible sigh of relief as he finished his report!

Almost the final smuggling fling in the area occurred in March 1853. The Customs Board received reliable information that a Lowestoft vessel, the *John and Susannah* had 'gone overseas for a cargo of tobacco, which is destined for the Yorkshire coast'. The collectors at Hull, Scarborough and Whitby were duly informed and ordered to keep a strict watch for this vessel. On 30th April it duly arrived in Whitby and was subjected to a most intense rummage – ten officers worked day and night to uncover the tobacco. Finally they found 5,037 pounds of tobacco cleverly hidden behind bulkheads. According to the officer's report, 'Immediately on the discovery being made, the master, James Bray, swore violently that "he had been sold out" and he jumped overboard into the harbour trying to drown himself but he was rescued with the greatest difficulty by my men'. The master and

114

the mate were each fined £100 and carted off to York Castle. Their subsequent petitions to the Customs Board were refused because they would not divulge to whom the tobacco was to be supplied. There were strong rumours amongst the Customs officers that a fish curer in Staithes was involved, indeed he had been suspected as being an agent for smuggled goods but there was insufficient evidence to bring a case against him.

The correspondence in this case seemed to go on interminably, almost everybody wanted to get in on the act. An Excise officer at Ipswich maintained that he should have a share of the seizure reward because he had passed on some of the original information, but his claim was quickly turned down on the grounds that this was part and parcel of his official duties. The real informer, who came from Lowestoft, received about £100 for his part in the affair but he considered this payment sadly inadequate and he continually petitioned the Customs Board for more money. All his appeals fell on deaf ears but then in desperation he wrote that 'my life is in danger from the smugglers'. The man, who was never named, caused the Customs Board so much trouble that in the end they offered to pay his expenses to emigrate to Australia! This offer was refused by the informant on the grounds of his age and that he had a sickly wife, but he added '. . . I think Portsmouth or Southampton is the more suitable place for me . . .'! In the hope of ridding themselves of this annoyance the Customs Board agreed and paid him £50 for 'travelling and settlement expenses' but he did not move away because five years later he was still pestering the Yarmouth Customs collector for 'a secure post that will offer me protection from my enemies'! I think it most unlikely that he ever obtained a Customs post.

As the century drew to a close, in fact almost on the last day – 30th December – a Newcastle vessel, *Mary Harrison*, which was on a coasting voyage from London, was found to have 375 pounds of tobacco hidden under coal. The Whitby collector said that the master had admitted that he had obtained the goods from a large Dutch smuggling vessel that was hovering just off the Yorkshire coast supplying colliers and fishing vessels. In almost 200 years nothing seemed to have changed!

Places to visit
Whitby is the perfect centre to tour and explore the North Yorkshire coast. A most delightful harbour still has much maritime activity and the old town nestling under the Abbey heights will give you a feel of how the town and port would have been in its whaling and smuggling days.

The town has ample places to visit starting with **Whitby Museum**, Pannett Park, a fine independent museum with collections displaying the history of Captain Cook, the maritime history of the port and the Scoresby whaling family. Open 10 am to 6 pm Easter to October and from 9 am to 4 pm from October to Easter (admission charge). **Museum of Victorian Whitby,** Sandgate, which recreates the town and port in its heyday of whaling and smuggling. Open at 10 am from Easter onwards, (admission charge). The **Captain Cook Memorial Museum**, Grape Street, a charming old house set in the old part of the town. Open Easter to the end of October daily. Weekdays only in the winter season (admission charge).

To reach Robin Hood's Bay, take the A171 Scarborough road and then at Low Hawkser the road to the Bay. The car park is situated at the top of the Bank and from there you can walk down the steep hill to Way Foot at the bottom of the village. As you explore the numerous narrow alleyways and lanes you can imagine yourself in the days when the Bay was perhaps the most famous smuggling village in the whole of the north of England.

Visit the **Smuggling Experience**, which is open from Easter to the end of October daily from 10 am to 6 pm (admission charge).

After leaving the village rejoin the A171 to Scarborough and travel about 7 miles until there is a left-hand turning to Ravenscar, where there is a National Trust Coastal Centre which has an exhibition featuring all aspects of the coast including the old alum workings. Open April to the end of September. The centre provides a range of booklets for children and teachers including one devoted to smuggling.

5
Scarborough to Spurn Head:
'From the Wykes to the Flats'

Petard Point is about two miles south of Ravenscar along the
Cleveland Way and provides an excellent vantage point to admire
the exhilarating stretch of coast, which has been aptly called the
'wyke and ness country'. The old path that winds its way along the
top of the cliffs was trudged by many a Coastguard man and it
passes Hayburn Wyke, a delightful wooded valley now a nature
reserve. From the sheer and breathtaking cliffs of Claughton Wyke
it is possible, on a good day, to see Filey Brigg in the far distance.
But what really commands the view is the massive headland of
Scarborough with its heights surmounted by the ruins of the
medieval castle lording itself over the old town with its neat but
busy harbour. Either side of this majestic promontory are the long
stretches of sands which have proved such an attraction to summer
visitors for over two centuries.

South of Scarborough stretch Cayton Sands, a delightful beach
which is another summer favourite as well as being the scene of
many a landing of smuggled goods. From thence all the way to Filey
is an unbroken line of cliffs well sprinkled with caravan and
camping sites proclaiming its attractions to holidaymakers. Then to
Filey Brigg, a natural reef of gritstone extending out seawards, the
most easterly point of the Yorkshire coast; this very unusual feature
proved a great hazard to shipping in the days of sail. Close by can
be found the old boundary of the North and East Ridings, which
now also sees the end of the Cleveland Way. Filey Bay is a
magnificent sweep of coast some six miles in length and has an
attractive blend of broad sands, high cliffs and small neat bays.
Those at Thornwick and North Landing have all the necessary
attributes of perfect smuggling coves – firm sandy shores
surrounded and protected by chalk headlands offering numerous
natural caves, many with reputations of their use in smuggling days.

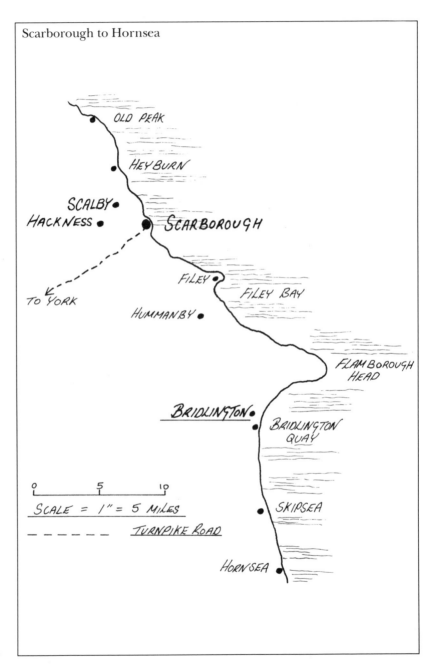

Scarborough to Hornsea

OLD PEAK

HEYBURN

SCALBY
HACKNESS

SCARBOROUGH

FILEY

FILEY BAY

TO YORK

HUMMANBY

FLAMBOROUGH
HEAD

BRIDLINGTON

BRIDLINGTON
QUAY

0   5   10

SCALE = 1" = 5 MILES

SKIPSEA

TURNPIKE ROAD

HORNSEA

North Landing, Flamborough: a well-known smuggling spot.

No visitor to this part of the coast can fail to be impressed by Flamborough Head and its great white cliffs, the old chalk beacon tower, the lighthouse and the superb views out to sea. Not surprisingly an early Coastguard station was sited there and the whole area well merits its designation as a Heritage coast. A broad beach of pebbles and chalk extends to Bridlington, with its harbour nestling securely in the lee of Flamborough Head.

From Bridlington to Spurn Head is some 35 miles in length, an almost continuous stretch of sand and sand dunes which has a special character all of its own. Very isolated in the heyday of smuggling, its coastal villages – Skipsea, Hornsea, Aldeborough and Owthorn – all had their brief claims to fame or notoriety during the days of free-trade. Their names figured frequently in the Customs records and reports of the time.

The whole stretch of this delightful coast is about 60 miles long and comprises virtually half of the total Yorkshire seaboard. It also provides all those natural features – cliffs, sands, caves and bays – which make the whole area so attractive to so many summer visitors. For a coast so steeped in maritime history it is perhaps 119 not really surprising to discover that it played a significant role in the days of smuggling, one that is not quite so well known as that of the coast to the north, not necessarily because it was less active but largely because its trade is not so well documented. Unlike Stockton, Whitby and Hull, the Customs records for its major port, Scarborough, have not survived, at least for the main smuggling years. Lacking such a prime and rich source of contemporary material it is necessary to look elsewhere and try to piece together the story from a variety of other sources.

There is no doubt that this coast had a long and age-old tradition of trading outside the strict letter of the law. As early as 1300 it was reckoned that 'merchants and others daily ship by stealth in the county of Yorkshire . . . and other merchandise liable to customs and export the same without satisfying the King'. The Exchequer records for 1278 show that seven men including the Prior of Bridlington (the Priory church still stands as a reminder of the Augustinian monastery founded about 1115) were alleged to have taken 164 sacks of wool to the port of Filey without informing the Customs. Then 20 years later a Peter de Blake was arrested when he tried to ship 70 sacks of wool through the same port. There was quite a furore in 1388: the Sheriff of Yorkshire supported by a troop of his men rode into Beverley to investigate illegal shipments of wool but they were roundly assaulted by the merchants of the town, who were most determined that no Crown official was going to interfere in their profitable but illegal activities.

In Tudor times Filey was said to have three pirates, Bridlington had seven whereas Scarborough boasted no less than twenty two! In those days the term 'pirate' covered a multitude of sins from harrying and capturing shipping, plundering wrecks and wool smuggling – indeed these so-called pirates were prepared to undertake any illegal activity provided it brought them some profit. Even the local gentry were not averse to underhand activities. In January 1603 Lady Margaret Hoby wrote 'This day [25th] it was told Mr Hoby that a ship was wricked [wrecked] up at Burniston [near Scarborough] upon his land and thus at all times God bestowed benefittes upon us. God made us very thankfull'! Such incidents show that at least there was a strong propensity for illegal activities, which came to the fore in the guise of free-trading.

The first real evidence of smuggling along the coast is seen in 1700 at Bridlington when Richard Woolf was charged with illegally shipping malt to Rotterdam. This is the only instance, to my knowledge, of malt smuggling. Malt, an essential ingredient in the production of both beer and spirits, was first taxed in 1696, one of the new Excise duties introduced to help finance the war with France. This Excise duty was said to be 'only a temporary impost for the duration of the war', yet it survived until 1880 and formed the basis of Excise revenue for nearly 200 years. Of course when malt was exported it was liable to an export duty – then 1s per bushel (eight gallons). Despite three respectable men, including John Rickerby, a maltster, speaking in Woolf's defence, he was found guilty and sent to York Castle. Three years later his petition for release was agreed by the Treasury because 'he has learnt his follys severely'!

In 1721 there was a Treasury report concerning a letter they had received from 'Mr Elias Hanvers, who visited Scarb'gh Spaw for his health'. Hanvers complained of the '. . . quite noisome activities of the fisher people of that town, who do lande all manner of goodes, said to be tea, brandies and wines on the sandes . . . the Customes of that place do seem to encourage such evil practices, wch brings such insults to his Majesties' revenue . . .' Regrettably the collector's answer to these charges, if indeed he had a satisfactory reply, has not survived. The Customs Board some months later merely replied to the Treasury Lords that they had made a full enquiry into the matter and found the 'sitacion is not as described by the petitioner'! However one is tempted to suggest that there is no smoke without some fire.

Bridlington Bay was well used by smuggling vessels. There is a fine broad beach to the north of the town ideal for landing goods and Sewerby, as well as Bridlington, was a busy market town offering outlets for the smuggled goods. In August 1724 Captain Robinson, who commanded a small Customs sloop *Spy* from Hull, was patrolling in the Bay when he sighted a French dogger landing spirits along the shore. But in the far distance there was what appeared to be a large foreign snow (a large two-masted vessel of up to 500 tons). Robinson said that he tacked in close to the dogger and fired some shots without any reply. After the dogger's rigging had been damaged '. . . all of the crew except 2 boys escaped to the snow'. Robinson added '. . . the bay is much 121

The harbour at Bridlington circa 1900.

used by foreign vessels who land their goods with the help of the country people'. The French dogger *Le Monde* was brought into Hull with 56 half-ankers of brandy, though it was admitted by Robinson that '. . . many had been landed already'.

There is a smuggling story regarding Bridlington which has been frequently repeated. It was rumoured that a vessel arrived in the bay with its flag at half mast and the whole of the ship's crew then paraded through the town behind six men bearing a coffin. However, the funeral never actually took place as there was no body in the coffin, it was filled with tobacco! The goods were successfully landed and then distributed on to York. The use of coffins as a method of landing goods is a smuggling legend that is repeated around all parts of the coast. Indeed, in Caernarvon (North Wales) it was reported that a local undertaker always used coffins to move smuggled goods. I suppose that the very frequency of such stories must prove that there is some truth in them.

In May 1729, Walter Kettleby, the Customs Inspector for the east coast, arrived at Scarborough on his inspection tour. He later went on to Whitby and has left some interesting comments on the port:

'[Whitby] is a smart [busy] port with a commodious harbour giving ample quays for traffick with Hull, London, the United Provinces [Netherlands] and the Baltick . . . fishing is also to the fore . . . the Colltr has a neat little coble wch is used to patrol around the headland and down to Filey . . . while I was present in the port this coble brought in some brandies and ten from a place Scabie [Scalby] where it was concealed near the Shore though I am informed that there is a path well used by the countrie people to convey the goods inland . . . There are many fine sandes here about wch appear well suited to the illegal trade . . . To the south of this place is Hummanbie where the offr is ancient and lacking in the urgency and the Colltr is of the opinion that many goods are run on that coast . . . it is advised that the said Risden be subrogated [substituted] . . . it is my belief that the smuggling trade is not so lively as other parts of this coast but it is the opinion of the Colltr that an armed cruiser would suit this purpose . . .'

It is quite surprising that despite both the Whitby and Scarborough collectors voicing the need for an armed cruiser, no vessel was supplied to either port, each had to rely on the two Newcastle vessels and to a lesser extent the smaller Hull smack. Whatever were the reputations of the Newcastle vessels, it was ultimately acknowledged (in the 1780s) that strongly-armed Revenue vessels had proved to be the most effective deterrent to smuggling.

Hornsea's parish church features in a smuggling tale in 1732. Apparently the parish clerk was quite deeply involved with the smugglers in the area, so much so that he used the church crypt as a store for landed goods. One December night whilst he was arranging his stock of spirits, a particularly severe storm was blowing which ripped off the church roof; this so frightened the clerk that he was struck dumb and died a few months later. Certain local people who were aware of his illegal activities felt that this was 'Heaven's judgement upon him'! Of course the use of churches and churchyards for hiding smuggled goods was a common element along all smuggling coasts. The majority of clergymen condoned smuggling and in some cases even supported and encouraged it; Parson Woodforde in Norfolk was the most famous example purely because of the detailed diary that he left. A surprising number of Victorian clergymen were fascinated by the trade and wrote highly romanticised smuggling 123 novels – the Reverends Cobbold, Barham, Hawker, Blackmore, Baring-Gould and Forbes all figure large in such literature.

In the same year that the parish clerk had his stroke (I assume that was the cause of his illness) a well-known Hornsea smuggler was said to have been taken to London for trial, perhaps because it was felt that a local jury would not convict him. He was found guilty and duly hanged. It is reported that his body was shipped back to Hull and hung on the gibbet at Hornsea. During 1732 there were six smugglers hanged at Execution Dock, one of these was said to be a Yorkshire felon, John Francis. So perhaps it was his body that provided such a gruesome and macabre reminder to others involved in the free-trade. Although hanging in chains was the means whereby the State could express its revulsion of a criminal and his particular crime, it did not then have a place in law. Not until 1752 did a new Act prescribe it as a punishment for certain crimes – notably highway robbery but *not* smuggling. This Act was so unpopular that often the gibbet had to be studded with thousands of nails to prevent the removal of the body by either families or friends.

If the above event did take place it did not seem to have any material effect on the local smugglers, because in May of the following year the Excise made a seizure of brandy and tea 'taken from a barn near Leven'. The farmer adamantly maintained that he had no previous knowledge of the hidden goods. This excuse could have been genuine, as barns were often used as temporary storerooms. Leven was situated at the crossroads where the roads from Bridlington and Hornsea met on the way to Beverley, so the goods could have been landed at either place, though Hornsea would seem to be the favourite as it was only about seven miles distant.

The *Prince of Wales*, the Newcastle Customs vessel, under the command of its very successful commander John Bowen, was cruising along Filey Bay in June 1736 when it disturbed a smuggling vessel landing goods to a cluster of fishing cobles just off the North Landing. As soon as the *Prince of Wales* came within firing range, the smuggling vessel began 'to tack furiously to gain the gauge'. The chase was rather short-lived, a few accurate and telling shots from the *Prince of Wales* and the smuggling vessel gave up. It proved to be *La Marie* from Dunkirk and had on board only ten and a half half-ankers of geneva and just six of brandy.

Captain Bowen, disappointed with this haul, quickly despatched a boat under the charge of his mate (possibly William Saville?). Unfortunately no other goods were recovered from the shore but Bowen reported that his boatmen 'had received some abuse and insult from the fishermen of that place, as well as the mobb of unruly country people that had gathered there . . . They [the boatmen] durst not rummage properly as they were afeared for their lifes, such was the heat of the people against his Majesties revenue. A stronger force should go amongst them to treat them a lesson for this grave insult . . .' The place of this outrage or insult was said to be north of Filey – perhaps it was Hummanby Gap or even Cayton Sands. As there were no injuries to the Customs men, perhaps the incident acted as a timely reminder of the escalating violence of the smugglers and the 'country people'.

In 1744, the Customs Board sent a circular letter to all collectors informing them that smuggling was on the increase. I have no doubt that the Hull collector was already well aware of this sobering fact. Nevertheless he decided to take the opportunity to remind his officers of the situation by issuing an order, perhaps mainly for the benefit of those riding officers covering the Humber and Holderness coasts, who seemed to be bearing the brunt of the smuggling in the area. He pointed out that:

'. . . there have been several instances of runs along our coasts and you are commanded to show your utmost diligence in your duties to patrol regularly and to watch the known places of landing by day and night. All informations that you learn by way of business is to be conveyed to your superior officers at your earliest and at all possible speede. Further you are to patrol at irregular times of the day and night without consideration of your private business and you must strictly record such visits in your journal, which will be inspected by your superior officer. The Honr'ble Commsn'rs have noted the recent increase of the illegal and pernicious trade and they expect you to endeavour to bring this trade to its ruination . . .'

Despite this stern warning there did not seem to be a rash of seizures, perhaps the officers thought that they had heard it all before. Later in the same year an Excise sloop *Fortitude* brought into Hull a quantity of geneva (220 gallons) and 410 pounds of tea, which its crew had discovered along the Holderness coast near Owthorn. The goods had been hidden in dunes. The 125 commander, James Terry, believed that they had been landed from a large smuggling lugger which had been sighted working along the coast for the past week or so. Terry admitted that they had been unable to track it down as 'it was a strong sailor'. At this time the *Fortitude* operated out of King's Lynn though it was later moved to Great Yarmouth. Excise vessels were far fewer in number than their Customs counterparts and as a result had a longer area of coast to patrol, indeed at times seemed almost to have a free hand. Generally they proved to be quite successful and were often commanded with more verve and daring than most Customs vessels.

The whole of the Holderness coast appeared to have been deeply involved in the free-trade. In May 1750 one of the Bridlington officers received some information about a run that was planned near Skipsea. He and several colleagues watched and waited patiently on the coast for two nights without any joy, only later to be told that the goods had, in fact, been landed at Atwick – some three miles further south. One wonders just what the Customs man said to his so called informant, especially as he had spent two fruitless nights out along the shore. This was quite a well-known smuggling ploy used deliberately to spread false information either to known informers or by stealth to ensure that the Customs were safely out of the way watching elsewhere.

The new collector at Hull was none other than Walter Kettleby, who had been promoted to this prime and prestigious post in 1748. Shortly after taking up his appointment he expressed very strong misgivings about the inadequacies of some of his riding officers along the Holderness coast. In 1751 he wrote a rather forceful letter to the Customs Board with the express object of getting them dismissed and replaced by more vigilant men. Such Customs posts were held under the patronage of the Customs Commissioners and to a lesser degree the Treasury Lords. The collector at any port had very little say in most appointments except those of a rather minor nature such as boatmen, though they were allowed to nominate their own clerks. Kettleby, who must have known most of the officers from his days as Inspector, put his case to London:

'. . . Mr Stagg, the excise Supervisor and some other Excise officers of this Town seized at a place called Seathon [near Hornsea Mere]. . . 660 pounds of tea, which had been run out of a Smuggling cutter two

Nights before . . . This vessel it seems has been constantly Employed in this Trade since Michaelmas last, and has generally landed on the Coast of Holderness between Hornsea and the Spurn Point from when Except what the Consumption of the Country takes, it is carried by land to York, Beverley and great Quantityes We are told are brought right into this Town to the harm of the legal trade thereof . . .'

Kettleby went on to single out those officers he considered sadly lacking in urgency – Mr Gorward at Patrington, Mr Bee at Skefling and Barnabas Pickett at Hornsea. He castigated them for their 'idleness and lack of seizures'. Even their supervisor – Mr Wright – was not exonerated. Kettleby maintained that since Wright's appointment back in 1742 he had only made one seizure amounting to a mere 2¼ gallons of brandy; the other three officers had between them only seized 32 gallons of spirits, 330 pounds of tea, 168 pounds of coffee, 359 pounds of liquorice and 64 pieces of china over a period of no less than ten years. The collector further pointed out that as these four officers all resided in the area and 'the amount of landed goods cou'd not possibly Escap'd their Notice, if they were diligent and Active in the Execution of their Dutys . . .' Despite this outright condemnation of these officers there is no evidence that any of them lost their posts, such a situation was a continual problem in the Customs service during the 18th century. Indeed at many ports there was ample evidence of useless officers retaining their positions purely because they held the favour and patronage of important and influential people.

Perhaps in some mitigation it should be pointed out that the latter years of the 1740s had seen one of the fiercest and most active periods of smuggling yet. Certainly the number of smugglers who were convicted had greatly increased and hardly a week went by without the report of a smuggling trial taking place somewhere in the country, shortly to be followed by execution for those smugglers who had used firearms and violence in the pursuit of their crime. Horace Walpole, that famous commentator on 18th century life, wrote in 1752 'It is shocking to think of the shambles this country is grown. Seventeen smugglers were executed this morning'. A somewhat hypocritical view considering that it was strongly rumoured that his fine table and hospitality owed less to the Custom House than to the free-traders! Perhaps that comment was merely sour grapes but it is

127

known that when his father Sir Robert was Prime Minister he arranged with the Secretary of the Admiralty to have his wine brought up the Thames by Admiralty barge without the payment of duty at the London Custom House – rather akin to the Chancellor of the Exchequer being caught defrauding his income tax! Considering the extent and violence of the trade and the poor example set by their superiors one can somewhat understand the lack of urgency of these Hull officers.

In an attempt to improve the situation along the Holderness coast Kettleby proposed that 'a fast sloop be stationed at Bridlington to patrol the whole length of the Yorkshire coast from the Tees to the Spurn'. He pointed out that there had recently been seized 'a smuggling vessel, only 50 tons but a Prime Saylor, an excellent sea boat and Esteemed the best saylor that has lately come upon this Coast . . .' However, the Customs Board refused his application on the grounds that '. . . the trade has greatly diminished in the last year [1754] on account of the reduction of dutys . . . the expense of this vessel is therefore not justified at such a time . . .' To a certain extent the Customs Board were correct in their assessment of the smuggling trade. There had been a perceptible decline in smuggling up to 1756 at least, and the sales of legal tea and brandy increased during these years. But with the outbreak of war in 1756 duties were quickly raised, and as there were fewer dragoons available to assist the Customs the illegal trade flourished once again and really did not decline again until the first decade of the 19th century.

It is somewhat strange that Scarborough, which even by the mid–18th century had acquired a certain air of genteel respectability with its growing reputation as a health spa and sea bathing resort, should also be the scene of two of the most brutal and bloody incidents in the annals of Yorkshire smuggling. The two outrages, though they were separated by over fifty years, showed that the town that later claimed to be the 'Queen of the Watering Places' also had a much darker and more sinister side to its character.

The fateful day was 8th August 1768; in the early evening three Excise officers challenged and stopped a farm wagon travelling along the turnpike road from Scarborough to Malton. The actual place where the vehicle was stopped was Ayton, just about four miles outside Scarborough. The two men who were leading the

19th century engraving of Scarborough.

cart refused to allow it to be searched. They produced pistols and during the ensuing struggle one of the Excise officers was shot and died almost instantaneously. As the subsequent report graphically described the murder, '[the man] presented a pistol close to the breast of the said John Smith and killed him on the spot'. During the commotion the two smugglers managed to make their escape but not before they had been recognised by the other Excise officers. One was said to be Joseph Haines, a shopkeeper from Harkness, a village just a few miles to the north of Scarborough. He was described as '5′ 6″ and waddles in his gait' and it was he who had actually fired the fatal shot. His accomplice was named as Valentine Bailey of Brocksway (Broxey – a neighbouring village), who was described as being '5′ 8″ in height late of the York Militia and by trade a tailor'. The goods they had defended with such purpose and violence amounted to 30 half-ankers of geneva, 240 pounds of tea and a small quantity of coffee. Immediately the Excise Board offered a reward of £100 for any information leading to the capture and ultimate conviction of the two men.

129

Whether this sum of money, relatively generous by the values of the time, led to the capture of the two smugglers or not, the two men were finally taken. Haines was convicted of the murder of John Smith and executed at York before the year was out. Bailey was sentenced to prison for his part in the affair and even seven years later he was still incarcerated in York Castle. He petitioned the Customs collector in Hull for his release on the grounds that his family were suffering 'dearly for his folly as they are now kept at the goodness of the parish'. Bailey's petition was passed on to the Excise Board for their consideration; though the outcome is not known, it is unlikely that Bailey was released as there had been a number of brutal attacks on Revenue officers during the period. Several Customs officers had been killed including, in 1769, an Excise supervisor in Yorkshire. William Deighton, who worked at Halifax, was murdered just a short distance from his house, a murder ascribed to a large gang of counterfeit coiners operating in Yorkshire who were also said to be involved in smuggling. Deighton had spent a long time collecting evidence about the gang and was on his way to meet an informer when he was waylaid and killed. In such an escalating climate of violence no Revenue Board would be prepared to show any sympathy to convicted smugglers especially those who had used firearms; indeed Bailey was very lucky to escape with his life and not be executed as an accessory to murder.

This disturbing increase in violence by the smugglers urged the Customs Board to pressurise the War Office to release more troops to assist their officers. In 1769 the Hull collector was informed that he had been allocated 40 dragoons to be deployed at his pleasure. He placed ten at Bridlington, seven at Hornsea and two at Skipsea, but unfortunately they were not kept in the area long enough to make any serious impact on the smuggling scene. The following year we find the collector pleading with London for some replacements as 'the troops have been removed from this Coast'. By November a fresh detachment was stationed in the area but only stayed five months. The Hull collector (Joseph Coultrie) rather despaired at this policy, his bitter letter to London ended, '. . . with smuggling drawn to such heights on this coast, I cannot see that my meagre force of officers can hope to stem this evil trade. Only a permanent deploy of the military will bring order to such a dissolute area. I would only add that the loss to the Public Revenue is unaccountable'.

Samuel Mannings, who was the collector at Scarborough, must have expressed similar misgivings because he was informed in January 1772 by the Customs Board '. . . your comments have been laid before the Hon. Commnrs. and I am directed to inform you that an armed vessel for your port is not considered necessary as the Newcastle and Hull vessels have strict orders to cruise your coast. The provision of military assistance is not at the behest of the Hon. Commnrs. and the Secretary of State for War has deemed it not appropriate at this difficult time to apportion troops to support the Revenue . . .' The difficult time referred to must have been the growing problems in American colonies, where there was mounting dissent at the imposition of new duties and the vigorous collection of them by the Customs officers, culminating in the Boston Tea Party of December 1773. It was quite clear that whilst there was trouble in the colonies, the War Office would be most loath to detach any troops to help the Customs.

At this time the revenue collected from the Excise amounted to almost £5 million, nearly double the sum raised from Customs duties, and moreover the Excise needed far fewer officers. Nevertheless there were over 10,000 persons employed in both services – a fair percentage of the literate population. Despite all the attendant risks and the unpopularity of the work both services maintained a waiting list for appointees and at one stage the Excise had to close its books to fresh applicants. The Excise seemed to be more successful against smuggling – at least on the Yorkshire coast. During 1773 Excise officers seized goods at Filey, Bridlington and Hornsea, all fairly large quantities of geneva, tea and wines, whilst during the same period there was a scant number of Customs seizures.

The *Newcastle Courant* published a report in October 1774:

'On Saturday morning the Scarborough Excise officers seized on the Dunes at the Northward of the Town at a place called Scalbey, sixty-one half-ankers of Geneva and about 1½ hundredweights of Tea and Coffee with some snuff, which they conveyed to their warehouse in the town. The goods were concealed in the sandes, and covered with some planks within 150 yards of the sea.'

The cavity must have been rather large to take this quantity of   131 goods! It is doubtful that the Excise had their own separate warehouse in Scarborough, the port seems to have been too small to justify one. So probably the goods were transferred to the Custom House, which was then situated on Sand Side near the west pier of the harbour.

In December the following year it was announced that there would be an auction sale of condemned (seized) goods at the Custom House, Scarborough – quantities of brandy, black tea and geneva would be 'sold publically to the highest bidder in several lotts suited as well for the use of private as well as a public dealers'. The goods could be 'reviewed before the Sale during Custom House hours'. The opening hours of Custom Houses had long been a bone of contention with merchants and shippers. They were from ten in the morning until two in the afternoon and the number of days the Houses were closed came to a grand total of 45 days a year! It was not until 1806 that the opening hours were extended to four in the afternoon and the holidays were drastically curtailed to ten days.

The year 1777 saw a most notable Revenue victory at sea. The large smuggling schooner *Kent*, with George Fagg in command, had been most active along the whole of the Yorkshire coast but Fagg seemed to favour Filey Bay. In April the *Kent* had been seen just off Whitby by Captain Mitchell of the small Hull cutter *Swallow*. Then on 3rd May Mitchell spotted a large fleet of colliers about '6 miles north-west of Spurn Point', the convoy was sailing south from the Tyne to London. As Mitchell closed on the fleet, he was dismayed to find amidst them the dreaded *Kent* busily supplying smuggled goods, and there was also 'a goodly gathering of fishing cobles'. Fagg made it quite clear to Mitchell that he should sheer off and as Mitchell later explained 'we did by reason of their superior force but we did our level best endeavours to spoil his market'.

However, Fagg's smuggling days were already numbered. In June a large barque arrived in Leith from London and reported to the Excise officers that the crew had seen a 'large smuggling cruiser with an accompanying lug-sail trading off Flamborough Head'. The Excise collector at Leith sought permission from his board in Edinburgh to despatch the two Excise vessels under his control to the Yorkshire coast to tackle this large smuggling vessel (at that time the Excise were unaware of the vessel's identity).

Considering that the Scottish Excise had only three vessels to patrol the whole of the Scottish coast, it was quite a risky decision to detach two vessels to Yorkshire. Nevertheless the order was signed and the *Royal George* and the *Prince of Wales* set off south.

The *Royal George*, commanded by Captain John Ogilvie, was a large (127 ton) ex-smuggling cutter *Fox*, it had an armament of twelve guns and a crew of 30 men. The *Prince of Wales*, captained by Lewis Gillie, was a newly built brig of 136 tons with 15 guns and a crew of 35. Without doubt these two vessels were by far the largest and heaviest armed Revenue vessels in operation in the whole of the country. By some strange coincidence virtually all the vessels that served both Scottish Revenue Boards bore royal names. Perhaps the Scottish Boards were more royalist than their counterparts south of the border, or maybe it was felt that because of the political position in Scotland their vessels should outwardly proclaim their royal authority!

On 11th July 1777 the two Scottish Excise vessels found their adversary and as expected it was the *Kent*, sighted just off Filey Bay and slowly progressing in a north-westerly direction. The sea was calm and there was barely a breath of wind. The *Royal George* managed to close within hailing distance, Captain Ogilvie identified himself and called out for the vessel to heave to or 'we will fire into you'. It was reported that Fagg replied in characteristic terms 'Then fire away you bouggars and be damned to you'! The battle commenced at ten o'clock in the morning with the *Royal George* firing away to the port side and the *Prince of Wales* to the starboard. As there was so little wind the three vessels were just drifting along and they were very close to the shore. For almost three hours the fierce fighting continued, watched by crowds of people lining the cliffs, it was even said that fishing cobles put out to sea with spectators so that they could enjoy a closer view – there would be no doubt which side they were supporting! The *Prince of Wales* took the brunt of the *Kent's* accurate gunfire and suffered some very severe punishment, its bowsprit was completely shot away and much of its rigging badly damaged. Because of its larger sail area the *Kent* could take the best advantage of the slight breeze; it was slowly slipping out of the range of the two Excise vessels and there was a real risk that it would escape once again.

However, a Naval frigate, HMS *Pelican*, attracted by the sound 133 of the guns, slowly hove into view and then proceeded to try to cut off the escape of the *Kent*. Fagg had two boats out towing his vessel in a brave but vain attempt to outdistance the new threat. Throughout the day the movement of the two vessels was painfully slow and at times it seemed touch and go whether the *Kent* would evade capture. By ten o'clock in the evening the *Pelican* managed to get within range and a fresh battle ensued, which according to all reports lasted throughout the night. Certainly Fagg was putting up very stiff resistance and making a real fight of it. But by dawn another Naval vessel, HMS *Arethusa,* appeared on the scene and the crew of the badly damaged *Kent,* seeing the futility of any further resistance surrendered to the Naval vessels. When the *Kent* was boarded Fagg and five of his crew were dead and the surviving 39 men impressed into the *Arethusa*. The two Excise cutters brought the battered *Kent* into Hull along with its cargo of some 190 half-ankers of geneva and 554 oilskin bags of tea. The vessel was ultimately sold for £1,405 and the guns, firearms and large stock of gunpowder finally found their way into Hull fort. The collector asked for the *Kent* to be refitted and brought into Crown service but he was informed most clearly that the seized vessel rightly belonged to the Scottish Excise Board! The apportionment of the various seizure rewards between the Scottish Excise and the Navy took almost two years to be finalised. Nevertheless this was probably the most successful joint operation ever completed as normally relations between the Revenue services and the Navy were never very cordial.

Rather strangely, in May 1779 there was another example of a successful Naval and Customs operation. The two Newcastle vessels *Mermaid* and *Eagle,* along with a Naval frigate HMS *Medea* tracked a smuggling cutter from Folkestone called *Friends Goodwill* right along the Yorkshire coast. It was first sighted hovering off Whitby near Robin Hood's Bay, later just off Filey Bay before it was finally cornered in Bridlington Bay. The subsequent fight was short, sharp and very effective, several broadsides from the *Medea* and the *Eagle* hardly bringing any reply from the *Friends Goodwill* before it lowered its sails in surrender. The spotsman – Richard King – was adamant, 'I did not strike to the Custom House cutters but to the *Medea*', obviously he did not feel so ashamed! The smuggling vessel was under the command of Richard Major (from Dover) who said that the real master was William Lawrence

134

who was ill at Folkestone. Major also wanted to make it very clear that 'we were determined not to strike to the Custom House cutters'!· The vessel had on board over 1,000 gallons of brandy, geneva and rum, as well as quantities of tea and coffee. Captain Whitehead said that his information was that the vessel had been using Filey Bay for the past 18 months.

One of the most notorious spots along this particular stretch of coast was Hummanby Gap, not very far from the site of the now disused Butlin's holiday camp. A rather amusing story about Hummanby appeared in the press on 15th April 1777:

'A few days ago a Person in Pudsey bought some goods that had been run and landed at Hummanby, on his return home to Pudsey, hearing that some officers were in pursuit of him, he sent for an Excise officer of the town to his own house and thereto delivered to him 66 pounds of black tea and 64 India handkerchiefs that he had obtained illegally.'

There were not too many of his kind around in those days, although there was another individual who did harbour a slight twinge of conscience at buying smuggled goods. He was a William Ogle who lived in Flamborough and kept a rather precise notebook cum diary. The entry for May 9th 1783 reads:

'Paid Rachel Woodhouse for 9 quarts and one pint of wine, wch she said had been found at sea in the fishing nets, was this really lost and how much duty was paid on it?'

As there are no further references to such transactions perhaps William Ogle had second thoughts on the matter of smuggled goods. Maybe these two somewhat reluctant customers had heard the strong words that the evangelist, John Wesley, used when he preached against smuggling. Wesley was one of the very few prominent persons to condemn smuggling outright. He constantly proclaimed that it was 'an accursed thing'. Such was his hatred of the trade that he refrained from drinking tea because such a large quantity was smuggled! He even published a pamphlet at his own expense wherein he maintained that 'every smuggler is a thief/general, who picks the pockets, both of the King and all his fellow subjects. He wrongs them all'.

On 23rd September 1779 the Hull collector sent an urgent letter   135 to the Custom House in London by post horse (he was later admonished for incurring such expense). The letter contained 'the latest intelligence from a Mariner belonging to the brigantine *Good Intent*, which arrived from Rotterdam'. It would appear that this vessel had fallen in with a French ship of war which carried 50 guns, also in attendance was a frigate of 36 guns and a small brig of twelve guns. The *Good Intent* was captured and its master and several of the crew were taken on board the French man-of-war. Then a small prize crew was put on the *Good Intent*, including an Englishman who had been a prisoner in France and had entered the French service to obtain his liberty. This Englishman with the remaining members of the crew managed to retake the *Good Intent* and bring it into Hull. Only then did the collector realise that this French squadron was commanded by the much feared John Paul Jones and that the Admiralty should be informed of the strength of Jones' force. Aboard the flag-ship were 600 marines and it was Jones' avowed intention 'to burn all the towns along the Yorkshire coast'.

Just one year earlier this famous American commander had played havoc with English shipping along the west coast of the country. The small Customs cutter the *Hussar* from Whitehaven had managed to escape undamaged after a long sea-chase that lasted nearly six hours. Then in May 1779 the Newcastle collector was warned by London that 'a foreign squadron under the American privateer was likely to be off his coast'. This information was quite accurate as Jones had raided Staithes for fresh provisions for his vessels. The two Customs vessels of the port, the *Mermaid* and *Eagle* were detailed by the collector to guard the port of Newcastle. Judging by their past performances one wonders what the Customs vessels would have done faced with the very professional seamanship of Jones?

Alas, the collector's letter of the 23rd was a little late with the news of John Paul Jones because by the evening of that very day the French squadron had been engaged in a battle by two Naval vessels HMS *Serapis* and HMS *Countess of Scarborough*. If the fight with the *Kent* two years earlier was exciting and impressive it paled into insignificance compared with the fierce sea-battle of the 23rd. So close were the vessels to the shore that it was said that some of the cannon balls grazed the cliffs at Flamborough Head where many spectators had assembled to watch the mayhem. The

Paul Jones: the battle off Flamborough Head.

outcome of this battle has now passed into history, and although it lasted barely three hours it proved to be most destructive and bloody. Finally the two Naval vessels were forced to strike their colours and on the following day Jones's flagship *Bon Homme Richard* sank from the severe damage it had sustained. The large Baltic convoy which had been one of the objectives of the French squadron sought refuge under the Scarborough batteries and ultimately reached Hull safely. John Paul Jones with his two prizes finally arrived at Texel in the Netherlands in early October. But for about two weeks the whole of the Yorkshire coast had been plunged into a state of anxiety and fear.

However, the excitement quickly died down and smuggling was soon back to normal as is seen in a report that appeared in the *Newcastle Courant* in 1780:

'It is reported that within the last week [August] at least two foreign vessels have been trading brandy, geneva and tobacco along the shores south of Burlington [Bridlington] in the County of Yorks. The Customs officers have been active in the area and have seized a quantity of the run goods but it is thought that the Country people have transported the goods far to the interior of the County.'

There are no references to seizures around Bridlington but two Scarborough Excise officers did uncover brandy, geneva and tea from an outhouse near Lebbertson, which is a mile or so north of Filey. The goods were thought to have been landed by 'a certain Osbarton from York City, who has for some time employed this   137 place to store his goods. Pray that part of this reward be paid to our informant as he is a poor and destitute creature . . .' Unlike much of the smuggling trade to the north of the county, which was kept firmly in the hands of the locals, a feature of the trade around Filey, Flamborough and Bridlington was the greater involvement of persons living a fair distance inland – York, Leeds and Thirsk. A rather strange and unusual snippet of news appeared in the *Leeds Mercury* in 1779 announcing somewhat archly that a Thomas Kent 'who was born in Kirksgate in this town and had previously travelled as an Auctioneer and sometimes as a smuggler on the coast of Hornsea and Filey yesterday se'night [week] procured a pair of pistols from a shopkeeper here . . .' One wonders why this information was thought worth publishing? Kent would have been already known to the Excise authorities because in 1777 an Excise duty was introduced on auctions and all auctioneers had to register with the Excise, paying a licence fee before they could hold an auction. Certainly by this newspaper notice Kent had become a marked man.

Such was the state of smuggling in the early 1780s that the Customs Board issued a strong letter to all their collectors. It was dated 5th January 1782 and is worth recording in full:

'The Enormous Increase of Smuggling, the Outrages which it is carried on, the Mischiefs it Occasions to the Country, the great Discouragement it Creates to all fair Traders and the Prodigious Loss the Revenue Sustains by it. We are most desirous to give a Great Cheque to this National Evil, but are much dismayed by our officers want of success in making captures, this Defect would not have been so if the Instructions and Orders given by this Board have not been duly observed. We therefore enjoin you to carefully peruse these Orders and ensure that the officers apprehend their contents unless they ignore them at their peril.'

There is no evidence that this exhortation to greater urgency with its threatening caveat had any appreciable effect on the number of seizures. Perhaps it might be worth commenting that smuggling looked vastly different viewed from the safety and comfort of a seat in the London Custom House compared with the reality of facing the fury and violence of the smugglers on some lonely cliff top or beach in the dead of the night. Considering the meagre pensions paid by the Customs Board to widows and to officers seriously injured in the line of duty, it is not really surprising that the majority of officers opted for caution and circumspection as the most sensible and safest course of action. However, the Board members and their officials, all of whom had obtained their positions by patronage, viewed such action as cowardice.

Nevertheless there were many brave officers who operated against quite overwhelming odds and often suffered grievously for their dedication to duty. In the very same year a rather strange measure was introduced by the Government which offered a free pardon to smugglers who would enter the Navy. If that was unattractive to them, they could provide a substitute to serve in their place and still be given a free pardon! That really sounds like a piece taken from a Gilbert and Sullivan opera!

Without doubt there was a paucity of seizures during the period leading up to the turn of the century. The *Eagle*, which was based at Whitby for a short period, did have some moderate success. In 1790 it brought in the small collier *Two Brothers*, a Stockton vessel caught landing ten bales of tobacco, 20 half-ankers of brandy and twelve canisters of tea just south of Scarborough. John Bland, the commander, said that the goods had been obtained from a large Dutch smuggling schooner that had been sighted 'near the Head' (Flamborough), and then three months later (in July) the cutter's boat crew searched the beach to the north of Flamborough, possibly Thornwick Bay or the North Landing, where they uncovered ten half-ankers of brandy, two of geneva and some bags of tobacco hidden near the cliffs. Perhaps these goods were secreted in one of the many caves that line the shore.

During one of the many interminable Parliamentary debates on smuggling, a lord expressed the view in 1805:

'It is impossible totally to prevent smuggling; the interested motives of mankind will always prompt them to attempt it especially when taxes are extremely high, and the hope of very large profits is a temptation sufficient to make light of any risk; all that the legislative can do is to compromise with the crime which, whatever laws may be made to constitute it a high offence, the mind of man can never conceive as at all equalling in turpitude those acts which are breaches of clear moral virtues.'

A defeatist or maybe a realistic view? Certainly not a particularly   139

The rocks and caves of Flambrough.

encouraging outlook and not one likely to raise the morale of the
Revenue services. But there were signs, albeit very faint, that the
worst of the battle was over; maybe at long last the Customs
service was beginning to assert its authority along the coasts.
Undoubtedly the very presence of preventive boats at
Scarborough, Filey and Bridlington had produced a restraining
influence on the smuggling trade, though their early results were
less than spectacular. Their value purely as a preventive measure
can never be properly assessed but nevertheless it should not be
totally ignored or underestimated. In fact the Bridlington
collector felt in 1820 that the preventive measures introduced in
the port had made 'a marked difference to the trade with the
chance of conviction being, at long last, a real fear . . .'

There is an amusing anecdote recorded in the *Memorials of
Scarborough* about an old lady in the town who recalled the 'good
old days of smuggling' of about 1810 or thereabouts. She said that
many a valuable cargo of contraband spirits which had been
landed between Scarborough Castle and Robin Hood's Bay
found its way into various houses in the town. She herself had run
numerous kegs of gin to places of safety in the town. Another one
of those doughty Yorkshire ladies who greatly relished the
excitement that smuggling provided!

140

Despite what the Bridlington collector had said about the state of smuggling in his area, the *York Courant* reported in December 1821 that a smuggling cutter had entered Bridlington Bay and was carrying '300 tubs of gin as well as tobacco and silks'. Now according to the newspaper report the Customs boat went out to intercept the vessel but finding that all the smugglers were over six feet tall the officers decided not to challenge the cutter! About a week later the Bridlington collector wrote to the newspaper rather indignantly. He wondered how anybody knew what the cutter was carrying because the Customs had not been able 'to get within a mile of her because of the heavy seas and thus had not sighted any of the crew'. In other words he firmly rejected the report as there was no basis for the story.

Scarborough was once again the scene of a most brutal incident that occurred as the direct result of a seizure of smuggled goods. In August 1822 the Scarborough preventive men received information of a proposed run to the north of the town. They gathered on the shore in some force and duly seized a large quantity of geneva, but, what they really wanted was the name of the ringleader and a William Mead from Burniston was persuaded to come forward and name a James Law, a wool merchant at Stainton Vale – some five miles inland from Scarborough. It seems that Law was already known to the Customs as being involved in the smuggling trade but on this occasion he stoutly maintained that he was not the culprit. Finally his case was heard in the King's Bench in London in December of that year and Law eventually won the decision; he was pronounced not guilty and Mead was found guilty of perjury.

This favourable outcome emboldened the Scarborough smugglers to take the law into their own hands. In January their anger was first directed against the Customs. Robert Maw, the Customs officer most directly involved in the case, had his house attacked by an angry mob. Then a month later John Dobson, a woodman from Pickering who had also informed against Law, was 'violently and viciously assaulted' whilst visiting the town on market day. He had several ribs broken then was tied to a ladder and dragged through the town semi-conscious and bleeding heavily. It seems that Law was present at the start of the assault and may have incited the attack with shouts of 'damn him, kill him, he is an informing devil . . .' Then some time later Law

141

along with others arrived outside Mead's cottage in Burniston threatening him with the same treatment. Mead, already frightened by the news of Dobson's attack, opened his bedroom window and fired a pistol at Law. One shot hit Law in the chest, from which he later died. The next day another one of Mead's friends, who had also given evidence for the Customs, was attacked by an angry mob said to number over 100, who left him almost for dead. The same mob again attacked Maw's house, and they tried in vain to break down the doors.

William Mead was arrested for the murder of Law but nobody came forward to give evidence as to the attacks on the other two informers. Mead's trial took place in York in July 1823 when evidence was given by a local girl that she had warned Mead of threats Law had made on his life, a fact that probably helped his case. He was found guilty of manslaughter and given two years hard labour – an amazingly light sentence considering the climate of the time. Rather wisely Mead never returned to Scarborough but is said to have followed a very successful career as a confidence trickster in Leeds. This incident showed how close to the surface was the violence associated with smuggling.

The newly-formed Coastguard had some considerable impact on the smuggling scene in Yorkshire. In 1826 they discovered 172 half-ankers of brandy and geneva and three casks of tobacco at Speeton Cliffs, just a few miles south of Hummanby. Then in the early summer of the following year John Andrew, the doyen of Yorkshire smugglers, was finally caught landing a consignment near Hornsea. He was found guilty and fined though it is not known just what penalty was imposed; figures vary from £1,000 to £100,000. The latter figure seems absurdly high, indeed even £10,000 would seem a grossly unrealistic penalty. Whatever the penalty was, Andrew could not find the necessary money and he, too, ended up in York Castle and stayed there for two years until his release was negotiated by some of his influential friends.

The Holderness coast and Hornsea in particular seemed to be the last bastions of the old-style smuggling. In October 1836, 50 to 60 tubs of geneva were thought to have been run at Hornsea but the Coastguard men managed to recover 20 tubs from 'a store along the beach'. In this instance they were very quick to point out that although they had been on patrol on the night in question, there had been 'a very thick fog which had hindered the operation'. At this time there was a general order in existence which directed that any men serving at a station where a successful run of smuggled goods had taken place would not be considered for promotion or 'any mark of indulgence or favour'! Consequently station commanders were very loath to report any information they received of successful landings in case they might jeopardise their chances of promotion, and Coastguard reports of the decrease of smuggling have to be considered in this context.

In May 1841 the Excise officer at Hornsea found a note nailed to his door informing him that the *Susannah* was landing tobacco along the coast. He confirmed the story by talking to one of the local landlords, who added that he had heard that the tobacco was all taken inland to York. Though the *Susannah*, which proved to be a Grimsby vessel, was never caught at Holderness, four years later it was seized by the Grimsby port officers with 80 bales of tobacco hidden under its cargo. The master was sentenced to two years hard labour and his vessel was confiscated. The last known smuggling run occurred at Hornsea in July 1846 when a fishing coble from Hull was seized along with its cargo of tobacco (60 bales). The Coastguard men expressed the opinion that 'this trade is now mainly conducted along the Humber as the local people show a marked reluctance in the trade'.

The Scarborough Coastguard commander, when asked to comment on the state of smuggling in his area, could only instance a couple of seizures over the previous five years (1841–46). Some cigars had been picked up from one of the regular traders to the port and just some minor quantities of brandy and tobacco from the fishing cobles. He was prepared to state quite categorically that 'smuggling is now a dying trade, they [the fishermen] are not prepared to hazard their vessels. Though the vigilance of my officers will be maintained as I have been reliably informed that the price of spirits in France has been greatly reduced and this might induce a greater incentive to smuggling'. The Bridlington collector was probably more realistic in his appraisal of smuggling in 1851. He considered that 'no part of the coast of England affords greater facilities for smuggling than the coast of this district and to prevent this trade requires a strong force which keeps the shore under constant supervision'.

A Revenue cutter in action, in hot pursuit of a smuggler's vessel.

Places to visit

Scarborough, as befits a premier seaside resort, has an abundance of attractions for the visitor. Of special note are:

Bygone and Maritime Scarborough Exhibition and Lighthouse Tower, which records the maritime history of the port. If you are feeling active it is possible to climb to the top of the lighthouse, situated at Vincent Pier at the harbour. Open from June to September (admission charge).

Quite close by is **The Three Mariners Inn**, a former smuggling inn just at the back of Sandsend which tells the story of smuggling and displays its various hiding holes. Open 11 am to 6 pm from Spring Bank Holiday to September (admission charge).

Shortly after leaving Scarborough by the A165 to Bridlington take a minor road to the left which will bring you to Cayton, an old smuggling village. After returning to the main road, some two miles later take the A1039 to Filey and follow directions to the sea front. At the north end of the promenade is a car park near the lifeboat station, known as the coble landing. From where in the summer months boat trips can be taken to view the Flamborough caves from the sea.

The village of Hummanby is reached from a junction off the A165 to Bridlington. There is a minor road to the car park, where a short walk will lead to Hummanby Gap, a well known landing place in smuggling days.

Again on the A165 and just beyond Reighton take the B1229 to Flamborough. If you wish to visit North Landing for some impressive scenery and cobles drawn up along the beach, take the B1255 just before the town. To drive right out to Flamborough Head with its lighthouse, Chalk Tower and Coastguard station take the B1259. The lighthouse is open daily (except Sundays) from 2 pm until one hour before sunset.

From Flamborough take the B1255 to Bridlington and follow the signs to the harbour; there you will find excellent displays of the history of the port. The old town with its 17th century High Street and Market Place, set about a mile or so from the harbour and modern resort, is well worth a visit.

Take the Hull road out of Bridlington (A165) for about six miles before branching off to the left along the B1242 to follow the Holderness coast through Skipsea, Atwick, Hornsea, Aldeborough, Owthorne and Withernsea – all well known as landing places in the days of smuggling.

To visit Spurn Head take the A1033 Hull road from Withernsea and at Patrington follow the B1445 to Easington. From thence the land is owned by the Yorkshire Wildlife Trust and an access charge is made for cars, varying from season to season, to continue along the Head.

6
Hull and the Humber
'From Hell, Hull . . . Good
Lord deliver us'

The Humber, for so many centuries a major commercial waterway, is a long inlet some 37 miles distant from its source at the confluence of the rivers Ouse and Trent to its entry into the North Sea. It is eight miles broad at its widest point and to each side of the estuary is an unrelieved prospect of flat and low-lying land, a mixture of sandbanks, salt mashes, mud spits and a myriad of small and winding creeks and shallows. The Humber has always had a rare reputation as a difficult and demanding stretch of water to negotiate, its navigation channel is particularly narrow and a vicious tide-rip in excess of seven knots thrusts around Spurn Point and races up the estuary. With such conditions it is not very surprising to find the early establishment of the Humber pilots (in 1512) in an attempt to reduce the number of vessels that regularly went aground along its shores.

The general aspect of the Humber estuary today is sadly very largely industrial; huge container vessels and oil tankers ply their trade to the busy modern ports of Grimsby, Immingham, Goole and Hull and the rash of refineries and chemical works at Paull have all somewhat marred its scenic attractions. Yet undoubtedly one of the estuary's most redeeming features is the Humber bridge, which was opened to traffic in 1981. This quite splendid single span suspension structure crosses from Barton to Hessle and replaced the several ferries that had served the estuary since the days of the Romans or perhaps even earlier. Surely it must be one of the most dramatic bridges in all Europe.

Today it is rather difficult to visualise just how the Humber estuary appeared in the heyday of smuggling or indeed when

William Bligh (of *Bounty* fame) undertook his famous survey of the estuary. Spurn Point, however, has hardly changed since those days. This rather strange spit of land some three and a half miles long was in 1676, the site of one of the earliest lighthouses in the country. The Point is now an internationally renowned centre for the study of bird migration. Paull, well up the Humber, was not only well known in smuggling days but also had a fine reputation for shipbuilding and perhaps the most famous vessel to leave its yard was HMS *Anson* – a large 44-gun man-of-war – which cost over £140,000 to build in the mid 18th century. One of its commanders, Captain Charles Middleton, was the son of a Customs collector, as indeed was William Bligh.

In the 18th century Hull was a small, compact town and port, still largely confined within its medieval boundaries – a tight assemblage of narrow streets, lanes and alleys. The landing staiths lined the Hull river and 'The Harbour', as it was known, was no more than a half-mile in length, stretching from the medieval harbour in the north to South End at the entry to the Humber. Across the narrow river from the town stood the Garrison. There was an age-old seaman's adage 'From Hell, Hull and Halifax, Good Lord deliver us'; whether this was indicative of the port's reputation in the 18th century is not really known!

Hessle and North Ferriby were both well separated from Hull in those days and deeply involved in the free-trade. It was at North Ferriby that two vessels believed to be over 2,000 years old were excavated – further evidence of the ancient maritime heritage of the estuary. Goole, some distance up the river Ouse, has more modern maritime origins dating from 1826 when the Dutch Canal was cut to link the Ouse to the industries of the West Riding; variously called the 'Venice of the North' and 'The Port in Green Fields', it is certainly the most inland port in the whole of the country, almost 50 miles from the North Sea.

The *Victoria County History of Yorkshire* quotes a Calendar of Closed Papers for 1354 which states

'Uncustomed goods might be shipped in Hull itself but more often smuggling took place from remote creeks along the Humber, it was for noticing and arresting a ship carrying wheat and lead to Zealand smuggled at some such 'hidden place' that the mayor and bailiffs of Hull were rewarded with £5 by the King in 1359.'

147

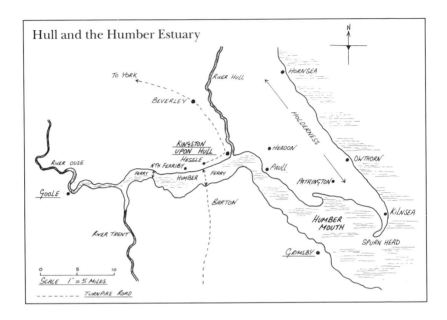

Hull and the Humber Estuary

Which proves beyond doubt that there was a long tradition of smuggling in Hull and along the Humber estuary. Prominent amongst the early Customs collectors of Hull were members of the de la Pole family. Richard rose from collector in 1322 to become the Chief Butler of England. His younger brother William started as a clerk in the Custom House, later became collector and was appointed the first mayor of Hull. His son Michael was Customer of the Port and later created Earl of Suffolk.

Certainly it was known that large quantities of wool were shipped 'by stealth each year to the Northern Provinces [Holland] for the small creeks and harbours'. So serious were the frauds that a senior Exchequer official was sent to Hull in 1417 to investigate. Some of his findings were most disquieting; it would appear that York and Beverley merchants were regularly shipping wool to Holland 'without customs'. They used any creek or small harbour to avoid going through Hull. In the past, two Dutch vessels had been seized for loading wool with Customs approval and a certain Henry Notte of York, a well known wool merchant, had travelled across in a Dutch ship to make contacts with agents in Scheidam. During the 16th century the President of the Council of the North maintained that corn was being regularly shipped out of the creeks of the Humber without any duties being paid.

By 1698 the owling trade (illegal export of wool) had reached new peaks, over 120,000 packs of wool were reported to be illegally shipped annually. Drastic action was needed and thus a 'landguard' of riding officers was established with two operating from Hull to cover the Humber estuary and the Holderness shore. But there was also another pressing and urgent problem – a large increase of smuggling around the coasts, and Charles Godolphin (Customs Commissioner for 1691 to 1714) was given the task of solving the problem. In August 1698 he proposed a scheme for the establishment of sloops 'for the better guard of the coasts to prevent the running of French goods during the high duties'. This proposal gained the full support of the Customs Board and was readily approved by the Treasury. Within the next twelve months Revenue vessels were established at ports right around the coast and Hull was provided with its own vessel appropriately called the *Humber*.

The limits of the district or station wherein the vessel was to patrol were clearly defined and it was emphasised that only in unavoidable circumstances, such as stress of weather or the chase of suspect vessels, should the vessel stray from its proper station. The *Humber* was to patrol the estuary north to Flamborough Head and to the south as far as Ingoldmells Point (just north of Skegness). The commander was reminded that the vessel should patrol ceaselessly and not stay in port longer than was absolutely necessary. He was also required to keep a journal to note and record all the day-to-day activities; this document would be inspected monthly by the collector.

It was in May 1710 that Captain Worthington, whilst on board the *Humber*, reported a rather strange incident at Skeffing:

'. . . t'was 4 after noon, we espied a boat in distress near the flats, on nearing it was seen to be a smugler landing goods to the shore wh're the countrie people were gather'd. We stop't their game not without some injury to the men . . . Brandies and tay were brought into the Custom House . . . The vessel was sunk by its master and the master and his men made their scape over the flats before wee could prevent the same . . .'

This is the one and only record of a smuggling master actually destroying his own vessel and shows the extreme limits to which smugglers would go to prevent their vessels falling into the hands of the Customs.

There was also a four-man rowing boat established at Hull, although it is not recorded whether the vessel was a 'coble'. In 1717 the boat crew picked up 'brandies, coffee and drugges' at North Ferriby from a Dutch vessel which had come to the port to load corn. Then just two weeks later (in April) some half-ankers of geneva were found 'along the shore at Paull' which according to the report had been 'dropt overside by one of the legal Hollanders that come into this port'. This type of smuggling was frequently used in the Humber, the long sea approach to Hull was ideal for this kind of operation. Indeed it was claimed in a Parliamentary debate that French vessels sailed right up the Humber in search of customers for their goods, which were commonly brandy, tobacco, silks and playing cards. One Member of Parliament decried Hull and the Humber as '. . . the blessed haven of wrong doers where smuggling reigned without hindrance to the great detriment of His Majesty's Revenue . . .'

In 1729 the Newcastle vessel *Spy* was transferred to Hull. Its commander, Captain John Robinson, a most able and conscientious officer and certainly one of the better Customs commanders of the time, was in September of that year involved in a dispute over a seized vessel. Robinson had arrested a Dutch dogger *Margrid*, which had been caught landing goods near the Spurn. Robinson found 180 casks of brandy, 13 English guineas and £7 in English silver on board the vessel; the money was obvious evidence of payment for goods smuggled. For some unaccountable reason the Customs Board informed the Hull collector that Captain Robinson should be called upon to justify his seizure and that the seized goods should be returned to the Dutch master unless Robinson was prepared to undertake the prosecution at his own risk. Not really able to understand the Board's attitude in this matter (and certainly it does seem an open and shut case) Robinson replied rather indignantly:

'I'll not stand tryal on my own charge, and I sent Mr Grant, ye Dutch merchant's Solicitor, to know how he would propose to bring ye matter to an Amicable Agreem't. His ans'r shall be handed to your

Hon'rable Commrs. on whom I shall throw myself entirely, to be made clear of all Charge, litigious Cavill and law suit, for I have done no more than my duty in bringing ye vessell into your suspicion.'

Ultimately the vessel and the goods were released and returned to the rather fortunate Dutch master. The Customs men had more than enough problems making seizures without having to suffer such a lack of support from their superiors in London. It is my belief that the Dutch master had managed to gain the influence of some powerful lobby in London.

As a direct contrast the Excise officers did not seem to have the same problems with their Board of Commissioners. When in 1732 they seized a consignment of tobacco (422 pounds) and ten boxes of tea in a house in Chapel Lane, Hull, which backed off the High Street, the two officers involved in the seizure were praised by their collector and this commendation was endorsed by the Excise Board, '… Their diligence has been noted and is most praiseworthy…' The goods were thought to have originated from a Danish vessel which had brought timber into the port. The Excise officers had no prior rights to search this vessel as there were no goods on the manifest which were liable to Excise duty. Therefore a request was passed to the Customs to allow the Excise officers access to the vessel; however, the Customs collector refused on the grounds that '… my officers are more experienced in the art of rummage and do not require any assistance…' It all smacks of sour grapes! There is no evidence that any further hidden goods were found, or indeed whether the vessel was even searched by the Customs. Nevertheless this is the very first evidence of tobacco smuggling in Hull, a trade that was later to assume immense proportions and would survive well into the 20th century.

In 1745 a certain Captain Joseph Cockburn was called upon to give evidence to a Parliamentary Committee enquiring into the smuggling trade. At the time Cockburn was in charge of the Customs cutter at Boston but he admitted that previously he had commanded many a smuggling vessel and his early apprenticeship to the sea had been made with a smuggling vessel from Rochester in Kent. Cockburn was not the first or indeed the last poacher to turn gamekeeper!

Cockburn had much to say on the inner workings of the free- 151 trade and he told of at least one smuggling trip to the Humber back in 1738 which gained him a cool profit of 250%! It was a rather ingenious fraud. Cockburn took on board 2,040 gallons of brandy at Dunkirk and cleared his vessel out for Bergen in Norway, though of course he had no intention of going there. Instead he sailed for the Humber and there met by prior arrangement a York 'keel', a flat-bottomed boat used almost exclusively on Yorkshire rivers. The master of this York keel had obtained legal permits for the exact quantity of brandy Cockburn had on board; the half-ankers were then transferred to the keel and brought up the river Trent to Gainsborough where they were landed legally as if they had been brought down from York duty-paid. Cockburn maintained that this type of operation was frequently practised in the Humber as the rivers Trent and Ouse 'were so useful for the purpose'.

Cockburn intimated that the Humber was an 'open waterway for the free-trade, where the pickings were most profitable . . . one of the reasons for this easy shore was the lack of any proper protection at sea . . .' The situation was made worse during times of war by the secondment to Naval duties of many Customs vessels, some of which never returned. For instance the *Strickland*, an 86 ton sloop stationed at Hull, was transferred to Commodore Smith's squadron at the Nore and did not return to Customs duties until 1748, almost three years later. Shortly after its return the Captain, William J'ans, was fined £40 (four months' salary) for 'being lax in his duties and spending too much time in port'!

Smuggled goods appeared to be landed with impunity in Hull itself. In 1749 the wife of a master of a Hull vessel which had just arrived from the Baltic was 'intercepted on the quayside with a quantity of lace, ribbons and handkerchiefs hidden around her person' – it was not stated just how the goods were discovered! Then just six months later a Danish seaman was picked up trying to sell tobacco in a street almost directly opposite the Custom House. Indeed it was well known in shipping circles that Hull was a port where the merchants greatly supported and encouraged free-trade. As already noted, Hull was the only port in the country that had not been compelled to establish legal quays. Therefore the port's shipping fraternity almost felt that they were above the law. It was even suggested that the smuggling trade extended to such a bulky commodity as timber. These goods were landed at

152

dead of night when the Customs tidesmen were engaged elsewhere. John Holland, a yard foreman with Haworth and Stephenson, important timber merchants in the port, was implicated and later convicted of smuggling timber. In his defence he stoutly maintained that there was a large illegal trade in timber and sailcloth.

One further and added complication for the Hull Customs officers was that on most Hull vessels seamen were entitled to carry a certain quantity of goods, the amount of which was normally dictated by the ships' masters. This appeared to be an age-old custom and was called 'furthing'. These goods were for private speculation and could amount to some bolts of damask, the odd package of tea or tobacco, German china and a box or so of toys. The seamen, of course, considered such goods to be theirs by right and therefore not liable to Customs duties. There were frequent instances of such goods being seized, which led to much confrontation and acrimony. Walter Kettleby, the Hull collector, admitted in 1749 that 'this port is so open to the pernicious trade like no other port on the East coast. I would require a far greater number of officers to stop all the wicked practices that have grown up at this place . . .' Such comments, coming from an officer who spent much of his early career inspecting east coast ports, must be accepted as a valid summation of the port's reputation.

Even when the Customs authorities were well aware of the names of certain smugglers, they still had considerable problems tracking them down, capturing them and finally securing a successful conviction. In 1753 the Hull Customs had used 'all manner of means at Great Expense to obtain some information' on three known smugglers – Richard Johnson alias Richardson, Edward Churchill also known as Edward Edward and Stephen Stephens nicknamed Stephen the Quaker. These three seemed to specialise in tea smuggling though they were known also to trade in brandy and geneva from both Flushing and Dunkirk.

The information the Customs had bought suggested that the three men would be staying together in a riverside inn on the Ouse just about three miles north of York. On 3rd May the Hull Customs controller, two officers and three bailiffs arrived at the spot only to find that they were on the west bank of the river whereas the inn was on the opposite side! By the time they 153

The press gang was very active in both Hull and Whitby.

managed to cross the river the three men had made their escape and no smuggled goods were found. Early the following morning, acting on further information, they went to a local gentleman's house and uncovered quantities of brandy, tea and wines – all these goods said to have been supplied by Stephen the Quaker. As it was discovered that Richard Johnson had a warehouse in Manchester where he was known as Richard Jobson, it was decided to follow him to Manchester, where after two days he was found, arrested and brought back to York Castle to await his trial. Such determination was very unusual, a rare case of the long arm of the Customs reaching out successfully! The other two men were believed to have left the country and set up trading in Flushing, where they joined the rapidly growing band of fugitive English smugglers.

The most pressing problem for the Hull collector was the adequate protection of the Humber estuary. In 1765 he had to admit that 'the creeks and sandes are well-used by smugglers and traders [legal] alike . . . the smuggling vessels used in these waters are larger and more heavily armed than those in the south of the country and our vessel [Humber] is much too small to cope with such large vessels, it is slow and a poor sailor and urgently needs replacement . . . the armes at this Custom House are aged and worn . . .' In fact Customs seamen carried only cutlasses, the commanders and mates were issued with pistols as well. The normal provision for Customs vessels was 56 pounds of gunpowder and the same weight of pistol balls. As these were often in short supply there were frequent instances of vessels having to remain in port because of lack of gunpowder and shot.

Another reason for the lack of success of the Customs vessels was the poor quality of the seamen. Their annual wage of £15 had long been surpassed by merchantmen and privateers and the only advantage they held over other seamen was the freedom from impressment. This was an insufficient inducement to attract the better class of seaman and at many ports it became most difficult to man the vessels so commanders were forced to take the dregs of the port or convicted smugglers. For many years one of the main complaints of the Revenue mariners was the lack of any compensation for injuries received whilst on official duty. It was not until 1780 that the Customs Board recognised the omission and made an allowance of £10 per annum should any seaman lose an arm or foot, but for slighter wounds only the surgeon's bill would be paid.

To add a little substance to his request for a larger vessel, the Hull collector quoted some damning statistics. During the five years 1760–64 the *Humber* had only seized goods to the value of £1,576, whereas the vessel cost over £600 a year just to keep it afloat. The plan worked because in 1769 it was replaced by the *Prince of Wales*, which was only slightly bigger but with 13 men had almost doubled the crew. In its first year of operation it had seized nearly £5,000 of goods and vessels, though admittedly most of this sum came from just one seizure. In May 1770 the *Prince of Wales* captured a large Dutch smuggling vessel near the Spurn along with over £1,000 (at auction) of goods. Just five years later it was joined by the *Swallow*, again only slightly larger than the *Prince of Wales*, and both these vessels were considered 'too small to compete equally along this coast'. Would the Customs Board never learn?

Perhaps some of the contempt felt for the Hull Customs can be seen in the attempt, in November 1763, to rob the Custom House. Edward Burrow, the collector, was forced to report this 'shameful affront to the Public Revenue'. He explained that it was 'about 1 or 2 in the morning, a high ladder was placed over the highgates into the flagged area, from which they gained entry to the land-waiters room, next to the Long Room and the King's Warehouse. John Nicholson, the watchman, heard some noises and called out "bring here the fire-armes directly, here are thieves and robbers" and then he continued to talk as if his brother watchman or some other person were with him and running 155 about in a great hurry and with so much noise that he so frightened the robbers that they escaped . . .' Nicholson was granted £5 reward for his 'stout and brave actions'. There is no record of anything being stolen.

The variety of goods that were smuggled into Hull was quite staggering – salt, starch, soap, candles, sailcloth, spices, medicines, dice, playing cards, books, porter (stout), china ornaments, musical instruments, toys, shoes, human hair (for wigs) and paper. In 1764 a Dutch master was heavily fined for not reporting ten casks of vinegar! Perhaps it was no coincidence that in the previous year an additional Customs duty had been placed on foreign vinegar, making it almost as costly as wine. Then two years later the mate of a Hull vessel, the *Pearl*, which had arrived from Hamburg, was convicted of smuggling German china. This was thought to have been specially ordered by a Hull merchant and the name Standidge is pencilled on the Customs report followed by a question mark. Samuel Standidge was an ex-mariner who had quickly prospered and by the 1760s was one of the richest merchants in the port. It is an interesting thought that some now very valuable Meissen pieces might have originally been smuggled into the country. Because of the extensive smuggling of such goods as candles, soap and starch, the legal minimum size for imports was raised to 224 pounds. By this stroke of a legal pen any small quantities of these goods found on board a vessel, whether they were hidden or not, became liable to seizure. Such import restrictions already applied to tobacco, tea, coffee and spirits.

The suggestion that a prominent Hull merchant should be implicated in receiving smuggled goods was not that outlandish. In June 1777 a Mr Clapham, who was said to be 'a wealthy yeoman from Cottingham', was prosecuted for receiving smuggled goods. Clapham made a counter-information against two small farmers in the area. The two men admitted that they had been involved in smuggling, regularly dealing in tea and spirits that had been run along the Humber. It was said that they sold green tea for 6d a pound and geneva for 3s 4d per gallon. Clapham also accused the two men of sheep-stealing (a capital offence). His solicitor said that 'they were infamous people and had concocted some scheme with some of the Customs officers at Hull to extort money from Clapham by way of Exchequer prosecutions'. The whole case

Smuggling cartoon of 1814, which showed that smuggling was rife throughout the country and touched all classes of society.

seemed to be getting slightly out of hand – smugglers, sheep-stealers and blackmailers! The collector put the whole sorry tale in its context. He said that Clapham was very well known as a wealthy but covetous man who had brought the sheep-stealing charge purely to deter certain informers giving evidence against him. As far as the collusion with his officers was concerned, he had found no evidence to support this and maintained that Clapham had been prompted by malice and revenge due to some earlier disagreements with the Customs. Clapham was heavily fined and the two farmers ended up in York Castle for smuggling.

The *Prince of Wales* brought into Hull a small smuggling smack, the *Mary*, which had been found hovering off the Holderness coast with geneva, tea and tobacco on board, most of which had not been landed. The crew of ten were handed over to Captain O'Hara of the Impress Service in Hull. The Hull rendezvous had always been a most prolific source of manpower for the Navy; in the previous year (1777) it had pressed no less than 330 men, the majority of whom were rated able seamen. How many of these were smugglers is not known, but the Navy were always particularly pleased to receive smugglers as they found them fine seamen and very reliable, providing they were sent to a foreign 157 station well away from their old associates. Some of the better smugglers are known to have been rated petty officers.

The men from the *Mary* were placed on board the *Lively*, a Naval tender which would take them to HMS *Conquistador* at the Nore. During the passage down the east coast the smugglers managed to overpower the Naval crew and they seized the tender, sailing off to Flushing. The owners of the *Mary* then had the audacity to blame the Customs for the loss of their vessel! They maintained that the *Mary* had been outside 'the English limits' when seized and further that it had only been taken on erroneous information supplied by the Scottish Customs Board. Furthermore they alleged that the crew had been impressed 'merely to frighten them into a confession'. They ended their appeal by adding that the crew had 'very fortunately escaped impressment as they were completely innocent of any crimes'! It is a great pity that the record of the outcome of this dispute has not survived but I think it highly unlikely that the *Mary* would have been returned to its owners.

To claim that a smuggling vessel had been seized outside the legal limits was often used as a defence ploy. Very many smuggling cases rested on this evidence and quite often the smugglers were given the benefit of doubt. For this reason the Revenue commanders were given very strict instructions to take a full record of the course the vessel was steering when first sighted and then to keep accurate notes of any subsequent changes in course. When seizing a suspect vessel the commander was required to set two bearings on separate points or, if possible, features on land, these bearings then had to be checked by at least two other members of the crew in order that they could swear to the correct distance in court. The infinite trouble most commanders took over this instruction must have made it an onerous task when fully occupied chasing a smuggling vessel. Really one could say that most of the advantages were stacked in favour of the smugglers.

However, one must not assume that all smugglers were completely devoid of patriotic sympathies. In September 1778 William Williamson, who was the surveyor in charge of the Bridlington Customs, sent a most urgent message to his collector in Hull:

'7½ this morning [16th] a small French cutter has taken 4 or 5 small ships, 2 or 3 of the guns from the fort fired and the privateer has shorn off a little from the stream of the Head ... one of the smuggling cutters has supplied the fort with some gunpowder. There is no gunpowder to be got for the fort guns – 2 barrels of gunpowder is needed most urgently ...'

Quite a unique action by the smugglers but one wonders how the Bridlington Customs managed to explain why they allowed the smuggling vessel to get away? During the 1770s the Customs had the assistance of dragoons. Although many were stationed along the Holderness coast, seven troopers were placed at Hedon, four at Aldborough and ten at Patrington, evidence of the importance the Hull collector placed on the protection of the entrance to the Humber ... In August 1776 this deployment of the military proved to be a most wise decision when four Customs officers, aided by troops of the 4th Dragoons, seized 745 gallons of geneva, 890 pounds of black tea, 302 pounds of green tea, 595 pounds of coffee and 110 pounds of tobacco. This fine haul was discovered at 'a narrow creek near the Spurn and had not the military been in attendance the countrie people would have rescued the goods but at the sight of them they slipped away and were lost among the reeds ...' However, this seizure was only the tip of the iceberg as the Hull collector made very clear just a couple of years later:

'Very good quantities of prohibited goods have been run, spirits, tea etc are loaded into boats and cobles, which are guarded by a great number of armed men, who are totally defiant of the officers and the Country people, many of whom follow no employment but this illicit practice, are constantly in waiting and being armed with Bludgeons etc. and provided with horses immediately convey the Run Goods to some distant place. Vessels are generally of the cutter or lugger kind, wch we have reason to believe are often built in Kent and are generally between 70–150 tons with crews of 25–30 men ...'

An even deeper concern for the Hull Customs came to the fore in September 1787 when a Swedish vessel was seized in the port for having a quantity of wool on board which had not been entered at the Custom House and thus no duty had been paid on it. The master of the vessel made a full and open confession 159 impeaching several notable merchants in the port, whom he claimed had carried on 'this trade for some years past'. The mate went even further when he maintained that every Swedish and Danish vessel that came into the port not only brought in smuggled goods but also took wool out on every voyage. Although it was felt that the quantities of wool were trifling, there were no less than 20 to 30 ships of those two nations regularly using the port and making on average three or four voyages every year. If only half the Swede's claims were true, the amounts of smuggled goods were quite considerable.

To add to the collector's embarrassment at this disclosure of the sorry state of smuggling in the port, the local newspaper, the *Hull Packet*, picked up the story and fulminated against the Customs. They posed the pertinent question – just what were the officers doing about the situation? Indeed they even implied that some of the officers were involved in the smuggling trade. Then just two months later, in November, the editor returned to the subject with a report that no less than three vessels were lately seen at one time plying their trade off the Humber. It was claimed that the vessels 'glut the country with brandy, cheat the revenue and return loaded to France with the staple commodity of our Country. The price of long wool has risen dramatically lately occasioned by the smuggling carried on to France.'

Richard Harrison, who had been appointed collector in 1783, decided it was the right moment to petition London for an increase in staff, possibly because he considered this was the best way to pre-empt any rebuke from head office for the apparent parlous state of control in the port. He pointed out how much the trade had increased in the previous ten years; according to him the number of vessels using the port had almost doubled and more especially since the opening of the new dock (1778). Indeed, the dock itself had created extra work for his officers, regular patrols of the quayside and the warehouses had to be carried out and this meant that there were less officers for searching. Thus he painted a very good picture of his officers being stretched to their limit just to control the vast increase in legal trade, let alone the illegal trade. In fairness to him and his staff, the trade of Hull did increase fairly dramatically over the last decades of the 18th century, and he was trying to operate his controls with a complement of staff which had hardly changed in the last 50 years. However, it was to be another two years before he received extra officers – just three – which really did little to alleviate the smuggling situation in the port.

At the same time the Excise appeared to be moderately successful in Hull and its environs. During 1789 its officers made many seizures not only in the town itself but in the neighbouring countryside. For instance in March an Excise officer was on a routine visit to a chandler (candle maker) in Salthouse Lane when he uncovered 40 pounds of tobacco and six bags of tea hidden in one of the storerooms. The trader was 'persuaded' to admit where he had obtained the goods – doubtless the Excise threatened to take away his Excise licence so effectively putting him out of business. The smuggled goods had come from the mate of a Hull vessel *Jason* which traded regularly with Denmark and always brought smuggled goods into the port. Unfortunately the vessel had just left the port and the Customs were notified in case they wanted to give the vessel special treatment when it next came into port.

Then in May two Excise officers stopped a wagon that was on the Cottingham Road carrying a small quantity of tea and brandy. This seemed to lead directly to another seizure of geneva and tea the following day at a farm at Skidby. Just a week later, obviously acting upon information, some Excise officers discovered what must have been a store in a wood on the outskirts of Beverley; it contained 65 half-ankers of geneva and 16 bales of tobacco. It was believed that the goods had been transported up the river Hull directly from the port. The Excise kept a watch on the wood for the next couple of days but not a soul turned up, quite obviously the message had quickly got around.

Also in 1789 the Customs boarded a small keel from York in the Humber near Hessle. It was fully loaded with coal and after many long hours moving coal they ultimately uncovered 14 bales of tobacco and six casks of spirits. The master, Nathaniel Mason, was forced to admit that he had bought the goods from a Danish vessel in the Humber estuary. It is not known whether the keel was seized and condemned but about the same time the collector received a letter from London reminding him of the regulations relating to the breaking-up of condemned vessels. It appears that at some ports such vessels were being sold and 'old and worn vessels being destroyed in their place'. The instructions were said to be 161 clear: 'The ballast, masts, pumps and bulkheads are to be taken out, the decks stripped and ripped fore and aft, the beams cut asunder, the bottom planks ripped off, the keels cut into four pieces and the stern posts into three'. Quite a comprehensive job if the instructions were followed to the exact letter.

The Customs Board were so concerned about the state of smuggling in the country in 1791 that it was felt necessary to make a report to the Treasury:

'. . . smugglers in general have become more daring than ever, and more frequently assemble in numbers carrying arms and in disguise. Instances occur very often of officers being wounded, beaten, opposed and obstructed in their execution of their duty, particularly in their attempts to make seizures of run goods. Due to the laxity of the Courts, whose light sentences to the House of Correction only, or to serve His Majesty by sea or land for a limited time, are frequently proved to encourage smuggling . . .'

No evidence exists to show that the Hull Customs experienced any particular difficulties with the magistrates in the town, but it would have been unique as a maritime town not to have some problems in obtaining smuggling convictions. There was a rather amusing case in 1792 when a farm labourer from Patrington was charged and fined for being drunk and disorderly. He tried to excuse his behaviour on the grounds of 'taken too much smuggled spirits'! Quite amazing that he would admit to one crime in the hope of mitigating another, or perhaps he was well aware what the magistrates thought of smuggling? It was accepted that smuggled spirits, particularly geneva, came into the country well over proof and needed to be diluted to bring them to drinkable strength. Indeed, in September 1792, Parson Woodforde in his country rectory in Norfolk records in his diary that he spent one whole morning diluting and bottling his smuggled gin and brandy.

Almost on the first day of the new century – January 2nd 1800 – the Excise cutter *Viper*, which appeared to be operating from Boston at this time, brought into Hull a Dutch smuggling cutter that had been discovered hovering at the mouth of the Humber. According to the commander, Matthew Gunthorpe, much of its goods had already been landed to fishing cobles near the Spurn. Only 20 half-ankers of geneva, six bales of tobacco and three

Receipt for Assessed Taxes 1791, which shows the Hull Custom House and some of the more unusual taxes of the time.

packages of tea were remaining on board when captured. Gunthorpe also mentioned that a Customs vessel (probably the *Bee*) was close by when the Dutch vessel was taken but '. . . she ignored all my signals, tacked and stood in for port without offering us any assistance . . .' Gunthorpe probably hoped that the Customs vessel would have searched some of the cobles. Whether he made a formal complaint to the Customs collector is not known but this again emphasises the superiority of Excise vessels to the Customs. In fact Gunthorpe was probably the most successful commander (either Customs or Excise) of his day. In 1808 the Navy introduced a rather novel competition: they offered three prizes to Revenue commanders who transferred the greatest number of smugglers to the Navy in any given year. Gunthorpe won the first prize of £500 (equivalent to about £20,000 today). He was a most experienced commander, having served from 1783 until he retired in 1816 with sufficient capital (mainly from seizure rewards) to buy a large estate in Norfolk.

However optimistic the local Customs were of some improvement in the smuggling situation, the Treasury was alive to the dangers which would result from the cessation of the Napoleonic Wars, so much so that they issued a cautionary letter in 1814:

'. . . after so long a period of war in every part of Europe, many of the most daring professional men discharged from the occupation and adverse to the daily labour of agriculture or mechanical employment will be ready instruments of these desperate persons, who have a little capital and are hardy enough to engage in the trade of smuggling . . .'

Although elsewhere in England there was sufficient evidence to justify the Treasury's grave misgivings – some of the most violent and bloody smuggling took place in Kent and Sussex after this time – as far as Hull and the Humber were concerned there were no real signs of any substantial increase in smuggling activities. But as previously stressed, the absence of seizures did not necessarily mean that the extent of smuggling had been reduced. Nevertheless in 1817 the Hull collector, Charles Lutwidge, felt that he had 'certain informations that smuggling had materially declined in this port. This state of affairs has been brought about by the regular patrol of the Estuary by the Preventive boat and the greater vigilance of the officers along the coasts. I feel that this is a situation that is to be praised and as the trade of this port has grown very large of late and the opportunities to trade illegally have also increased . . .' Lutwidge, who served in the port from 1810–1841, came from a family steeped in Customs tradition; his grandfather had held a senior position in the north-west and his father had served in Whitehaven and Newcastle. One of the main reasons for the family's long connections with the Customs service was that they held the patronage of the Lowthers – a powerful and influential family in the north of England.

Lutwidge's rosy prognosis about the state of smuggling in the port seemed to be seriously flawed when just a few years later there was a sudden rash of seizures. The success of the Customs can almost be attributed to the energies of just one man – Captain James Gleadow. He was appointed Commander of the *Bee* in 1820 and was one of the few civilian commanders to be so appointed. Most commanders now came from the Navy, they were usually Naval lieutenants on half-pay. Perhaps the most famous was Captain Frederick Marryat, better known as a best selling novelist. His view of smugglers of the time was, 'Smugglers do not arm now, the service is too dangerous; they effect their purpose by cunning, not by force. Nevertheless it requires that smugglers should be good seamen, smart, active fellows and keen witted, or they can do nothing . . . All they ask is a heavy gale or a thick fog, and they will trust to themselves for success.'

Whether Gleadow held similar views is not known but certainly from his arrival in Hull the Customs seizure rate increased quite dramatically. On 19th June 1820 the brig *Friends* was boarded about three miles from Spurn Head and the first rummage of the vessel produced a large quantity of 'India handkerchiefs', opium, quicksilver (then regularly used as a medicine), snuff and two silk umbrellas. All these items were found hidden behind false bulkheads. The master of the vessel had 15 yards of silk concealed in his pockets as well as tea, tobacco and snuff hidden in various places in his cabin. During the following four days the Customs men continued to search the vessel, which by now had arrived in the dock at Hull. They found a further variety of goods – geneva, tobacco, currants, 'segars' (cigars), more handkerchiefs and quicksilver – and finally under ropes in the forecastle, a case of mirrors. By this time both the master and mate had disappeared; they were later said to be in Hamburg. It is interesting to note that the legal cargo of the *Friends* was bones – both human and animal collected from the many European battlefields. It must have been a most distasteful task for the Customs officers to rummage such an offensive and foul cargo.

This seizure just marked what seemed to be a one-man vendetta against smugglers. In the following two years the *Cossack*, from Denmark, was found to contain tea, coffee, cigars, playing cards, pepper, chocolate, and cloves – all hidden on board. Another vessel, the *Lord Wellington,* from St Petersburg, was seized along with large quantities of silk goods. Then two vessels from Hamburg produced a range of goods including, tobacco, playing cards and silk goods, most of which were found hidden in the cargo though cigars and snuff were discovered under 'the false bottoms of drawers'. A small sloop of just 42 tons, *Anna Thorina,* was rummaged whilst in dock and small quantities of tobacco and spirits were found in the hold but Captain Gleadow was firmly convinced that the vessel had already landed most of its illegal cargo in Bridlington Bay. His reasoning was that 'the little value of the cargo, the smallness of the sloop and the number of her crew being six, it cannot be thought that the said owner could sail his Vessel without the Illegal practice of Importing Contraband Goods'.

In April 1823 Gleadow took the *Bee*'s small gig up Crably Creek some 15 miles from Hull where he disturbed a group of smugglers unloading goods from a small smack. He only managed to arrest one of the smugglers – William Newell – but did secure most of the goods, tobacco and snuff. Newell was fined £100 and ended up in gaol, though his solicitor maintained that Newell had only gone on board to deliver a message and that he was 'a very poor man in embarrassed circumstances'. However, both Gleadow and the collector were convinced that Newell 'had for some time past been a notorious smuggler'. Although Newell was not released, he was awarded the poor person's allowance, which came to 4½d a day whilst in prison. This sum, paid by the Customs, was said to provide one and a half pounds of bread and one quart of beer. In 1826 the allowance was increased to 7½d a day but by this time the cost of living had so increased that there was no advantage to the prisoners; one prison reformer claimed that Crown debtors (mostly convicted smugglers) existed on a starvation diet. Things did not improve because in 1833 it was decreed that all prisoners (including debtors) would undergo hard labour, which meant that many had to walk the treadmill.

Despite his undoubted success Gleadow appeared to have great difficulty in obtaining his reward money for all the seizures that he had made. In 1825 he sent a petition to London enquiring whether there was any reason why he had not received any money for the previous two years. He also asked why the Excise Board seemed to reward its officers so much better than the Customs. I am afraid the answer was quite simple – it was commonly accepted that the Excise was a far better managed and more efficient service than the Customs, and it would be the mid-century before the Customs department was reformed and brought to greater public accountability.

It was during the various Customs reforms of the 1850s that a tide-surveyor at Hull was dismissed for corruption. Although he had an excellent record of seizures he had also been engaged in tobacco smuggling and at times was thought to have seized his own consignments to allay suspicion and happily allowed his crew to go to prison. Eventually there were the inevitable disputes over the share of the profits and he was informed on by certain members of his organisation discontented over their portion. After he was dismissed from the Customs service he was appointed harbour-master at Hull; perhaps the local merchants felt this was a just repayment for the many goods that he had supplied them duty free.

Punch magazine considered Coastguard stations as 'castles of idleness where able-bodied men spent their time looking through long glasses for imaginary smugglers', but this rather unkind and harsh view was far from reality; certainly the Coastguard along the Humber seemed to be active enough, there were many instances of seizures of smuggled goods (mainly tobacco). There were also frequent references to 'sunk' goods being found by Coastguard boatmen whilst they were on creeping patrols. One particular seizure near Patrington in May 1824 is worthy of mention. The Coastguard had received some information that a local carter operated 'a regular trade of tobacco to Hull'. Then four days later he was again intercepted at the very same place, and this time he had four bales of tobacco on board. Presumably he thought that lightning would not strike twice in the same place! From now onwards the most smuggled commodity in Hull and the Humber would be tobacco. In 1826 no less than 1,500 pounds was found in hollowed-out logs on a vessel in the docks, and two years later the Excise seized over 600 pounds of tobacco which was being pushed along the Holderness Road in broad daylight.

The steady reduction of import duties had made the smuggling of many goods no longer a profitable enterprise. The illegal trade in tea, wines and silks had virtually ceased by the 1830s. The only goods worth smuggling were spirits and tobacco and spirits, largely because of their bulk and smaller profit, were smuggled far less; so for the rest of the 19th century the main commodity of the smuggler was tobacco. A report issued in 1844, examined the conditions in the tobacco trade, and alleged:

'a considerable amount of tobacco is daily brought into the United Kingdom and can be obtained anywhere for 2s 6d per pound [the duty alone was 3s 2d]. Special establishments have been set up in Flushing and Nieuport for the express purpose of packaging tobacco for the smuggling trade . . .'

Much of the smuggled tobacco was brought ashore by ships' crews. A captain of a Boulogne steamship maintained that all his men smuggled tobacco; they were deliberately paid low wages 167 because 'they have the power to make a venture'. It was said that tobacco which could be bought on the Continent for £100 could be sold in Hull for nearly £1,000 if all went well. Many tobacco merchants said that they could not afford *not* to buy smuggled tobacco otherwise they would go out of business. As one reluctant Hull tobacconist admitted, 'I always hated smuggling. I was always in fear; from the beginning I only did it in self-defence'!

In 1844 the Customs received information about a Hull vessel called *Billy Boy* which, according to the informant, had left early in November ostensibly to obtain ballast at Spurn Point but instead had run over to Holland and loaded 140 bales of tobacco and tobacco stalks (used for the manufacture of snuff). This consignment had been illegally landed 'on the Humber shore without any problems and then transported into Hull and York with the greatest possible ease'. It was said that this consignment was shared by a Mr Charles, Michael Miller and the informant, who confessed that he had suffered from a severe bout of conscience because 'he was a strict churchman'. The same vessel made a second trip but, caught in a blinding snowstorm after a terrible passage, it was forced to lay off Grimsby for a whole day until the weather improved and then found that it had been lying alongside a Revenue cutter! The following morning the *Billy Boy* quickly got under weigh and landed its cargo at Stone Creek. The informant admitted that he had kept the cut tobacco but had sent the stalks to Leeds. He further asserted that he knew of several other vessels that landed tobacco (about ten to eleven tons each) either on the Holderness coast or in the Humber. Indeed it was his opinion that 'any quantity of tobacco can be landed at Hull' and that an American tobacco agent had offered a Hull tobacco manufacturer any amount of smuggled tobacco, '. . . leave your warehouse door open and we will take care the tobacco is placed there. If it is seized we shall not ask for any money; if it goes through safe, we shall ask you 2s in the pound in a banker's bill for two months payment . . .' – smuggling by mail order!

The general impression is that the Humber and Hull were wide open to tobacco smuggling with a sad lack of Customs control. Indeed the collector admitted in 1843 that he had 'no doubt that there were landings of large quantities of tobacco up the Humber and try as we may we have great difficulty in stemming this flow of illegal trade . . .' In the five years up to 1846 nearly 15 tons of

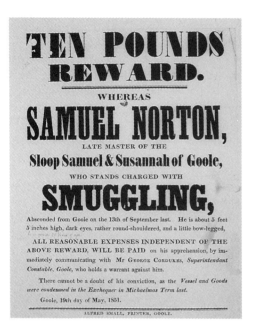

tobacco (33,600 pounds) had been seized in Hull and well over 250 persons convicted. The collector further estimated that perhaps the Customs only managed to seize less than 20% (probably a conservative estimate!), suggesting that perhaps tobacco in excess of 75 tons was being smuggled into the area – an enormous figure by any standards. An eminent London tobacco broker declared that from 8,000 to 9,000 tons of tobacco were being smuggled into the country annually; if this estimate was correct, such staggering figures made the earlier smuggling days pale into insignificance.

Much of the smuggled tobacco remained in Hull but some went further inland. There were frequent Excise seizures in Leeds, Sheffield, Thirsk and York. In March 1848 two Excise officers seized 'two horses, one wagon and 912 pounds of tobacco in the forecourt of York station' – it was being prepared for dispatch by train to Leeds! In this case the Excise firmly believed that the goods had been landed at Goole. There is a surviving poster of the period dated May 1851 offering a £10 reward for Samuel Norton, 'late master of the sloop *Samuel and Susannah* of Goole, who stands charged with smuggling'. He was described as 'about

169

5 feet 5 inches high, dark eyes, rather round-shouldered and a little bow-legged'. The poster also pointed out that there could be little doubt of his conviction as the vessel and the goods had been recently condemned in the Exchequer Court. However, Norton had decided to abscond, and unfortunately it is not known whether he was ever caught. These two examples show that although Goole was a very new port (1828) it soon became deeply involved in the tobacco smuggling trade.

And how did the Customs dispose of all this seized tobacco? Well, in November, 1852 it was directed that in future all seized tobacco (except cigars) should be destroyed by burning instead of being sold at auction as it was felt that the sale of tobacco on such a scale led to abuse and was unfair to the legal trade, 'by displacing in the market a corresponding quantity of tobacco which would have otherwise been entered for home consumption'. From those days special furnaces were built in Custom Houses for the purpose and the chimneys became known as 'The Queen's Pipe'! It is interesting to note, however, that during the Crimean War all tobacco seizures were sent to the War Office for use by the army in the Crimea.

With even further reductions in import duties after 1861, the only commodity regularly smuggled was tobacco. It was found hidden in a wide variety of goods from casks of potatoes, bales of hops and even in loaves of bread. In Hull there were examples of it being concealed in boxes of oranges, hollowed-out timber and in tea-chests – what a change from the days when tea was the main item smuggled. The Customs Board reported in 1875 that 'the temptation to smuggle offered by the high duties imposed on tobacco must always induce attempts to defraud the Revenue'. The continual increase in tobacco smuggling was a deep concern for the Customs; the duty from tobacco accounted for almost 47% of their total revenue and it was almost equal to the yield from income tax, which in those 'good old days' was a mere 6d in the £1. The tobacco trade in 1881 was not in a very happy position, as only three years earlier the duty had been increased by 4d to 3s 6d per pound. This duty increase caused great agitation in the trade, the 'obnoxious 4d' as it became known was considered grossly unfair as the commodity was already very heavily taxed (equivalent to 400% by value). It was felt that this duty increase would lead to even greater smuggling.

The Excise service was also involved in some rather large seizures of tobacco. In 1877 a paper manufacturer in Bradford had offered a tobacco merchant goods at a lower price than the duty. This merchant informed his local Excise officer, who accompanied by police searched the paper mill and found some 500 pounds of tobacco carefully hidden in large reels of paper. Information was also supplied about other premises in Leeds, where a further 1,500 pounds was discovered. The tobacco had been landed along the Humber near Paull and it was said that Hull was the centre of a very large tobacco smuggling operation. The regular tobacco merchants complained bitterly to the collector that their 'businesses were being severely injured by the scale of the illegal trade'. During April and May 1880 a unique combined operation was mounted by the Customs, the Excise and the police, resulting in over 13,000 pounds of tobacco and cigars being found in various premises in Cottingham and Hull. The fines imposed in this large smuggling case totalled over £25,000. The police became further involved in tobacco smuggling when they were issued with special commissions enabling them to seize uncustomed goods; however there is little evidence that they were very successful in Yorkshire.

Further large seizures by the Hull Customs were made in the 1880s. In 1882 over 6,700 pounds were discovered in a German vessel that was anchored in the river Hull 'just above the North bridge' and in May of the following year over 3,000 pounds of tobacco were found in a workman's hut on the banks of the Humber not very far from Hessle. These goods had been landed from an American vessel. A Hull man who was a former ship's steward with a long record of smuggling tried to escape in a nearby boat but was arrested, convicted and ended in York gaol. It was said at his trial that he had been one of the leaders of a large smuggling empire which arranged supplies of smuggled tobacco throughout Yorkshire and Nottinghamshire.

Besides such large seizures there were innumerable smaller seizures from crew members; the Dutch and the Germans were particularly adept at smuggling. It was said that 'the general use of steam has greatly increased the difficulties of the rummaging officers, spaces in connection with the machinery, which can only be searched when they have become cool, are becoming favourite places of concealment'. Judging solely on the Hull figures, the

171

number of engine-room men who were convicted of smuggling offences fully justifies this opinion.

One positive and practical step taken by the Customs Board in the late 1870s in an attempt to stem this illegal trade was the provision of steam launches to work in the large rivers and estuaries. In fact the Customs was the first public body fully to recognise the advantages of steam vessels for such estuarial duties; the first steam lifeboats did not come into operation until 1889. By that time a steam launch called the *Trent* had been in service at Hull for well over five years. This vessel, had according to the collector, 'proved an effective check on systematic smuggling by keeping a far closer supervision on the movements of vessels in the Humber'. Such was the success of this vessel that five years later another steam launch was supplied for the port, rather appropriately called the *Humber.*

By the beginning of the 20th century, the amount of tobacco smuggling had reduced considerably. In the Customs Board's opinion this was due to the increased vigilance of its officers, although they did add a caveat that 'the Humber still presents some problems with hard-core smuggling by the crews of steamers and fishing boats. The Hull seamen seem loath to forego their smuggling traditions'. However, the one constant problem in the north-east was the presence of Dutch coopers which operated just outside the limits and were thus free from British control or intervention. They did a fine and profitable business supplying large quantities of duty-free tobacco and spirits to the fishing fleets. Their very presence, and there were at least eight of them at any given time, 'was a constant source of anxiety to the Department [Customs]'. Even official complaints at the highest level to the Dutch government did little to help the situation. But in 1906 two of these coopers happened to stray inside the limits and were found hovering near the mouth of the Humber 'just south of the Spurn'. The Coastguard cutter *Argus* went out and arrested them both and they were brought into Hull along with the large cargoes of tobacco and spirits.

From the early years of wool smuggling to the more modern days of tobacco smuggling, Hull and the Humber estuary had been very deeply involved in the free-trade for well over 600 years – a considerable smuggling heritage that rivals any other port in the country.

172

Smugglers at work. (Langbaurgh on Tees Borough Council).

Places to visit

The City of Hull abounds with links to its past maritime glories.

Ferens Art Gallery, Queen Victoria Square, has many marine paintings and local views of Hull's thriving maritime past. Open Monday to Saturday 10 am to 5 pm and Sundays 1.30 pm to 4.30 p.m. **Town Docks Museum**, also in Queen Victoria Square, features whaling, fishing, trawling and the maritime history of the port. Opening hours as above. **Wilberforce House**, the birthplace of William Wilberforce, has some fine collections on costume and slavery. Opening hours as above.

The **Old Harbour**, which dates from the 12th century, is situated on the river Hull between Drypool Bridge and the Humber. It is still in commercial use and there are pleasant riverside walks along the old wooden quaysides.

The **Marina,** the former Humber Dock which finally closed in 1969, is now a modern complex of housing, shops and restaurants. It also houses the old Humber lightship, which is on view Monday to Saturday 10 am to 7 pm and on Sunday 1.30 pm to 4.30 pm.

Index